£25.22

 **the** **information** **store** ☎01603 773114
email: tis@ccn.ac.uk

21 DAY LOAN ITEM

2 3 FEB 2015

2 6 JUN 2015

Please return <u>on or before</u> the last date stamped above

A fine will be charged for overdue items

 CITY
COLLEGE
NORWICH

Cognitive Behaviour Therapy

An A–Z of Persuasive Arguments

MICHAEL NEENAN

Centre for Stress Management, London

and

WINDY DRYDEN

Goldsmiths College, University of London

W
WHURR PUBLISHERS
LONDON AND PHILADELPHIA

© Whurr Publishers 2002
First published 2002 by
Whurr Publishers Ltd
19b Compton Terrace, London N1 2UN, England and
325 Chestnut Street, Philadelphia PA 19106, USA

Reprinted 2002, 2003 (twice), 2004 (twice), 2005 and 2006 (twice)

British Library Cataloguing in Publication Data

A catalogue record for this book is available from the British
Library.

ISBN-10: 1 86156 326 4 p/b
ISBN-13: 978 1 86156 326 2 p/b

Printed and bound in the UK by Athenaeum Press Limited,
Gateshead, Tyne & Wear.

Contents

Preface

Helping clients to develop alternative and more constructive viewpoints to tackle their problems lies at the heart of cognitive behaviour therapy (CBT). This development is facilitated by the quality of the arguments – not to be confused with arguing – you present to your clients. Students as well as experienced practitioners frequently complain to us that they are 'stuck' when it comes to answering some clients' self-defeating thoughts and beliefs; they lack or cannot think of good and persuasive arguments to put forward at the time (one reason for this may be because they believe the same ideas as their clients). Echoing Hauck (1980a), we would suggest that your strength as a cognitive behavioural therapist is, in part, measured by your ability to summon up rational arguments to challenge clients' irrational arguments.

The purpose of this book is to provide you with some ideas and arguments that you can present and build on in your discussions with your clients. But just presenting ideas plucked from this book without further elaboration of them is hardly likely to promote client change. Therefore, this book represents an addition to your 'argumentarium' in the same way that new techniques are added to your armamentarium.

Cross-references in the text are shown in small capitals.

absolutist thinking

Absolutist thinkers view events in rigid, dogmatic and unqualified terms (e.g. 'I must get others at the meeting to agree with my point of view') and emotional disturbance is likely to occur when other people do not see things their way (e.g. the person feels angry when the meeting disagrees with his viewpoint) along with the unpleasant realization of how limited their power and control actually is. Absolutist thinking is extreme thinking (e.g. 'Either you love me or you hate me'; 'If I'm not a success, then I'm a failure') as the person omits complexity from his worldview and refuses to acknowledge that there is a range of viewpoints and options to consider within these extreme positions. Therefore, an absolutist thinker is unable to compromise or tolerate differences and is convinced of the correctness of his opinions.

Flexible thinkers, on the other hand, are less likely to trigger emotional disturbance as they do not have a preconceived view of how things must turn out or how others must behave; therefore, they have developed contingency plans to meet changing situations and can adapt to unanticipated outcomes. Flexible thinking is based on wishes, wants, preferences (e.g. 'I would very much prefer others at the meeting to agree with my viewpoint but there is no reason why they must agree with it') and is more likely to promote successful problem-solving and emotional stability than absolutist thinking. (In a play on Lord Acton's famous dictum that absolute power corrupts absolutely, we might say that absolutist thinking disturbs 'absolutely', e.g. 'I was absolutely furious with him', 'I'm absolutely appalled by your indifference towards me').

acceptance

Some clients refuse to accept that they have a problem because to do so would mean surrendering to it (e.g. 'The depression has won').

However, refusing to accept the problem can reinforce clients' daily difficulties and intensify their negative feelings – the only 'victory' they have won is a pyrrhic one. It is important to point out to your clients that acceptance is not a descent into resignation but the starting point for the constructive fightback against the problem. Now their energies will be focused on learning ways to ameliorate their problems instead of reinforcing them (see SELF-ACCEPTANCE).

achievement-driven

Achievement helps us to feel good and prove our competence in a particular area of endeavour. Compulsive achievement, on the other hand, usually stems from the need of the individual to prove her worth as a person, that she is good enough. Constant challenges are sought to feed her ego, which can never be satisfied as she is only as good as her last success (the 'glow' from each one quickly fades). Therefore, a compulsive achiever cannot rest on her laurels as she would see herself as a FAILURE if she is not continually striving for success.

In order to savour her achievements, the person should not make them an index of her personal worth, i.e. her intrinsic worth as a human being remains constant irrespective of what happens to her in life. Once she stops judging herself on the basis of her successes or failures, she will remove the compulsiveness from seeking achievement, and not be afraid of failing as she sees it as an opportunity for learning rather than self-condemnation. With this outlook, she will now be focused on personal growth, not constantly proving herself – in this way she can escape from what Burns (1981) calls the 'achievement trap'.

A–C thinking

In rational emotive behaviour therapy (REBT), this refers to people assuming that activating events (A) cause emotional consequences (C), e.g. 'Being stuck in traffic jams make me angry'; 'Talking to groups makes me anxious.' People who frequently make A–C connections in their thinking believe that their emotions are determined by factors outside of their control: they can only feel better when events change or people behave differently towards them.

However, A–C thinking fails to account for why people react differently to the same event. For example, failing an exam might lead to thoughts of suicide in one student, another is determined to retake the exam, while a third student says she is not bothered by the results. If events did determine our reactions, then the three students should all have felt suicidal, for example. To start understanding why we feel as we do about events in our lives, we need to pinpoint our idiosyncratic evaluations or beliefs (B) about these events rather than focus on the events themselves:

A = activating event - talking to groups and predicting that someone will ask a question I can't answer

B = beliefs - 'I must be able to answer all the questions asked of me because if I can't, this will mean I'm stupid.'

C = consequences - anxiety

Moving from A–C thinking to B–C thinking (i.e. our emotional reactions are largely self-induced) means we are responsible for the way we feel: 'Thus, emotions are not foisted upon us or inserted magically into us, but result from something we actively do. Specifically, emotions result largely from what we tell ourselves' (Walen et al. 1992: 26). Changing the way we feel by changing the way we think puts us in control of our emotional destiny, e.g. the person no longer feels anxious talking to groups because he stops insisting that he must answer all the questions and refrains from making his self-worth contingent upon answering all of them.

action vs. outcome

Some clients might believe that their actions show how helpless they are in the face of an outcome they can neither control nor alter (e.g. dying of cancer). This is to confuse action with outcome (Glover 1988). In the example, the client cannot change the grim outcome, but he can *choose* how he wants to live the last months of his life. In other circumstances, clients can attempt to influence outcomes but with no guarantee of success, e.g. a client behaves in a charming manner towards a woman he fancies, but she decides whether or not to go out with him. To believe he can make her choose the 'right way' through his actions might again engender a misplaced sense of HELPLESSNESS if she chooses the 'wrong way'. As Glover remarks: 'Only a thorough exploration of the boundaries as well as the scope of your field of choice and action will ultimately yield a more self-directed life' (1988: 124) (see RESPONSIBILITY).

addiction denial

Some clients may deny that they have substance abuse problems and are only attending therapy because of pressure from others (e.g. a partner, employer). It is important not to get into an argument with a client as to why he is refusing to see the obvious deterioration in his life and functioning but, instead, suggest an experiment to determine if there is a problem – will he give up the particular substance for the next seven days and see what happens without it? After all, he can spend the rest of his life using the substance, so what is a mere seven days without it?

The proposed experiment can induce anticipatory anxiety about the perceived 'horrors' ahead and the client may refuse or be reluctant to engage in it or he may abandon the experiment within a few hours or days of starting it. If there is no problem, why is it he was so fearful about engaging in the experiment or stopped it so soon? His reactions to the experiment can be the first step in the change process: acknowledging there is a problem. Then he can decide if he wants to tackle it.

advice-giving

When clients ask for your advice on how to tackle their problems, some of them may say at the next session, 'Your advice didn't work,' and thereby attempt to undermine your credibility or wait for you to come up with another suggestion because they expect you to carry the responsibility for their change. It is understandable why you might become defensive about the advice you gave (e.g. 'It usually works. I don't know what went wrong') but Hauck emphasizes that you 'do not get caught in this trap. Instead, immediately ask the client, "Well, why didn't you make my suggestion work?" or "What did you do that prevented my ideas from working?" In other words, make *the client* responsible for not showing any improvement since the last session. Don't automatically assume the responsibility' (1980a: 228; original author's italics). Examining the reasons for lack of progress might reveal, for example, the client's ambivalence about change or her aversion to the EFFORT required to achieve her goals. This is why your client did not make your suggestion work.

always and never thinking

A client might say after the break-up of her relationship: 'I will always be alone and I'll never be happy again.' Has the end of her relationship endowed her with the gift of prophecy? Her 'prophetic' utterance is based on seemingly invariant thinking (e.g. 'I will always see things this way and I will never change my mind') which, in turn, is derived from her current DEPRESSION and bleak outlook. Has the client made 'always and never' statements before and how accurate were they? Finding one exception to an invariant rule undermines it. Keeping a diary will help the client to determine the accuracy of her current predictions and realize that her thoughts, feelings and circumstances are in a state of flux rather than set in stone.

anger

When a person is angry, she changes from a democrat into a dictator. When she is in an unangry state, she believes in freedom of thought, speech and choice. When angry, she attempts to impose her will on others through a 'tyranny of the shoulds' (e.g. 'You shouldn't think like that'; 'You should keep your mouth shut'; 'You should only be interested in me, no one else'). As Hauck states: 'You don't run the world, and if you don't like the views [or actions] of others, change them through example and debate, not force' (1980b: 71).

The person can also be angry with external reality for not obeying her demands (e.g. 'I shouldn't have a flat tyre'; 'I shouldn't have bad weather on my holidays'). She is demanding that reality should not be reality and, if she is right, her tyre will spontaneously reinflate or the rain will suddenly stop and the sun come out. If she overthrows her tyrannical thinking by silencing the shoulds, then debate with others replaces demands on others and she learns to distinguish between what aspects of reality she can change (e.g. her flat tyre) and what she cannot (e.g. the weather).

anxiety

A person might believe that feeling anxious helps to keep him focused, motivated, maintains his high standards and enables him to meet his deadlines (e.g. 'The pressure keeps me on my toes'). However, his anxiety can also be inhibiting, impairing or incapacitating at times. The very emotion he sets so much motivational store by can also prove to be demotivating and demoralizing (e.g. 'I'm so anxious about the talk next week, I'm having second thoughts about doing it'). Instead of needing anxiety 'to get the job done', the person tries to achieve his objectives without piling on the pressure and compares the results between his anxious and unanxious (i.e. concerned) states. Does the pain and tension of anxiety add quality and polish to his finished work or performance or detract from it? Can he prove that without those sleepless nights he would not have finished the report on time? The next time he tells himself that he needs to feel anxious to get the job done, he should pause and ask himself: 'What does it really contribute to the process or outcome?'

apathy

Apathy can appear at first glance an appropriate coping response (e.g. 'If I don't care about the end of the relationship, then I won't feel depressed'). However, on closer inspection, affecting apathy is an attempt at SELF-DECEPTION, i.e. pretending not to care when the person really does. She might fear that expressing her true feelings about the loss of the relationship could lead to a deep depression or uncontrollable anger, so she tries to suppress these feelings. This strategy is usually unsuccessful as these unprocessed feelings continue to torment her and she becomes more, not less, preoccupied with the end of the relationship. Apathy can be viewed as an anti-goal as no constructive change occurs or is encouraged by the person.

A middle way between apathy and disturbance is for her to acknowledge honestly that she does care the relationship has ended, accepts its loss without engaging in catastrophic predictions (e.g. 'I'll never be happy or love again'), self-denigration (e.g. 'I'm nothing without him') or denigration of her erstwhile partner (e.g. 'He's a bastard for leaving me'). Then, if she chooses to, she can take steps to find a new partner.

approval-seeking

Excessive approval-seeking from others means believing 'I am what others think of me'. It is as if the person has put himself on the stock market as a commodity: his stock or personal worth is determined by whether others invest or disinvest in him. Even when he receives the approval of others, he never really enjoys it as he worries that the approval may be withdrawn at any time. His behaviour reflects his approval-seeking as he pleases others in any way he can. However, others are likely to take advantage of, look down on or reject him because they see he has no self-respect; he may also have a low opinion of or even hate himself for behaving in this submissive way.

The antidote to excessive approval-seeking is SELF-ACCEPTANCE: the person accepts himself, warts and all, irrespective of how others see him. With this outlook, he allows others to make up their minds about him without engaging in placatory or pleasing behaviour to influence the outcome. Acceptance is something we give to ourselves rather than given to us by others.

arguing

Some clients may frequently argue with you and, if you argue back, therapy slips into a power struggle with a winner (the client is pleased you are frustrated with his lack of progress) and a loser (you doubt your clinical competence). Sidestepping arguing with your clients shows them that your ego is not on the line and they can 'win' the arguments but they will also 'lose' because they will remain emotionally disturbed while you will continue to enjoy your life. Also, you are neither going to nor can you force them to do anything they do not want to do (they are in control of the situation because they can leave at any time or not come to the next session). The client's provocative statements can be met with an open-minded concern for his welfare:

Client: Therapy is crap.
Therapist: In what specific ways is therapy crap and how can we improve it in order to help you?
              or
Client: I'm not doing any bloody homework tasks!
Therapist: Okay. We'll review what you learnt from not doing homework at the next session.

By taking the wind out of your argumentative clients' sails with your non-defensive responses, you can help them to focus their attention on solving their problems instead of prolonging them through time-wasting activities.

assertiveness

Assertiveness is standing up for one's rights without anger (Hauck 1991a), but some clients believe it means getting what they want from others whenever they want it. This outlook often leads to anger when these others do not pay attention to them or fulfil their requests. Also, not being assertive all of the time signals a return to perceiving themselves as being weak or exploited. Point out to these clients that assertiveness is a considered response to a particular situation, not an automatic one in every situation in order to appear 'tough' or prove 'I'm not going to be pushed around any longer'.

Being selectively assertive means weighing up the consequences of one's behaviour and sometimes concluding that silence is more prudent than assertion (e.g. not jeopardizing one's promotion chances by being outspoken about one's boss). Being continually assertive can result in an 'assertive backlash. When people act on encouragement to stand up for their rights, they often find themselves fired, divorced or otherwise disenfranchised for having done so' (Robb 1992: 265).

An important benefit of assertion training is thinking and feeling differently: 'by letting other people see, through our behaviour, that we expect to be treated as a person of worth, we are also likely to affect our own evaluation of ourselves and what we are capable of' (Sheldon 1995: 203).

attitude selection

How we respond to events is largely determined by the attitudes we hold about them. Choosing an attitude to adopt plays an important part in how we deal with problems or view life in general. For example, one person may give up quickly when the going gets tough (e.g. 'I can't be bothered to struggle to find an answer') while another battles on to find a solution to her problems (e.g. 'I'm going to do whatever it takes to sort things out'). Though we bring prior attitudes to present problems, this does not mean that we have to continue adhering to these attitudes – have some of them outlived their usefulness or do they bring more costs than benefits?

Selecting a new attitude is not the same as selecting a breakfast cereal to buy: the latter is bought and consumed without much effort on our part while internalizing a new attitude requires a lot of practice and effort (e.g. repeatedly telling oneself 'I can stand it' while undertaking and completing boring or difficult tasks that were previously avoided). Choosing an attitude is applicable to every situation, no matter how extreme it is, as attested to by the late Viktor Frankl, an eminent psychiatrist who survived Auschwitz:

> We who lived in concentration camps can remember the men who walked through the huts comforting others, giving away their last piece of bread. They may have been few in number, but they offer sufficient proof that everything can be taken from a man but one thing: the last of the human freedoms – to choose one's attitude in any given set of circumstances, to choose one's own way.
>
> (1985: 86)

authoritarian epistemology (DiGiuseppe 1991)

This means believing that something is true because a credible authority figure says it is (e.g. 'My father told me that crying is an unacceptable weakness, so he must know what he's talking about'). Accepting uncritically what we are told by authority figures means we take on their ideas instead of thinking things through for ourselves – we become dependent-minded instead of independent-minded. It is advisable to take on trust what an expert tells us because we do not have the knowledge to challenge her (e.g. a consultant physician informs you that you have diabetes), but we should not automatically defer to an expert's opinions on subjects outside of her area of expertise (e.g. how to be happy in life) just because she is an expert. We may well conclude that some pronouncements of authority figures are true but this is based on our reasoning, not obediently accepting theirs.

Sometimes authority figures are not identifiable individuals (e.g. a schoolteacher) but the amorphous 'everyone'. When a person invokes the collective authority of 'everyone' (e.g. 'Everyone thinks the speed limit should be raised') to justify his own behaviour (e.g. speeding), he can ask himself how he knows *everyone* believes it. Even if a majority of people do believe in a particular idea, this does not make it true, legal or useful to the individual.

avoidance

Avoiding facing our fears may bring short-term relief but usually perpetuates these fears thereby diminishing our overall enjoyment of life. For example, fear of rejection may prevent a person from asking women out. This keeps him safe from hearing the dreaded 'No' but also keeps him locked into his unhappy solitude. Overcoming his avoidance by exposing himself to his fears helps him to: problem-solve rather than problem-avoid, tolerate the intense discomfort experienced before, during and after the event, encourage risk-taking in order to develop a more adventurous life, and enables him to re-evaluate his fears realistically instead of catastrophically (e.g. 'no' is only devastating if he allows it to be so). Giving up the protection of avoidance may seem counterintuitive but protecting ourselves against our fears makes us more, not less, vulnerable to them.

awfulizing

In rational emotive behaviour therapy (REBT), assuming that things could not be any worse than they currently are (e.g. 'My partner leaving me is the end of everything'). Awfulizing statements not only create emotional disturbance but also self-paralysis – if it is the end of the person's world, then nothing she does will make any difference, so why bother? Realistically, negative events exist on a continuum of badness (0–100 per cent), so what she believes is 100 per cent (the end of a relationship) is actually less – because where would she place on the continuum losing both legs in a car accident, being horribly burned, or her entire family being killed?

Anti-awfulizing is acknowledging that bad events could always be worse and therefore her personal world may have been severely battered but not shattered or brought to an end (e.g. what has not changed in her life since the unpleasant event occurred and what can she continue to do?). Also, anti-awfulizing allows for the possibility that some good can eventually come out of bad events (e.g. 'Since the relationship ended, I no longer take my friends for granted and have been closer to them than ever before'). It is important to point out to your clients that anti-awfulizing does not in any way make light of catastrophes (e.g. earthquakes) or personal tragedies (e.g. losing a partner to cancer), but underlines the inescapable point that no one is immune from experiencing grim events. Introducing awfulizing into these events adds nothing to relief efforts for earthquake survivors or coming to terms with the loss of a loved one: in fact, it will detract from these activities.

B

backsliding

Slipping back into self-defeating patterns of thinking, feeling and behaving is a common experience for clients, both during and after therapy, as they strive to internalize a new problem-solving outlook. Setbacks are a natural part of the change process as is the client's fluctuating confidence in her ability to maintain her therapeutic gains; therefore, backsliding should not be viewed as a failure but as an opportunity for learning. For example, a client who returns to alcohol use at times of interpersonal strife can pinpoint those factors, like fear of rejection, which continue to be a source of VULNERABILITY for her.

Helping clients to prepare for setbacks through RELAPSE PREVENTION programmes can be invaluable in reducing the chances of a future lapse (stumble) turning into a relapse (collapse). Anticipating that your clients will experience some setbacks is not to succumb to a philosophy of pessimism but is a realistic assessment of the likely progress of fallible (imperfect) human beings.

badness

Some clients might view themselves as 'rotten to the core', intrinsically bad, because they have, among other reasons, committed bad acts, believe they were born bad or were labelled bad by others. Being intrinsically bad means the person has no redeeming features and, therefore, he can only perform bad acts for the rest of his life.

This bleak view that the 'stain of badness' can never be removed from a person's character overlooks the fact that we have some measure of FREE WILL and therefore the person can learn to look at his bad behaviour in a new light. For example, bad behaviour does not make you a bad person, you are not what you do (the PART–WHOLE ERROR says that you are what you do). Teaching your clients to say 'It's bad' (e.g. failure,

11

theft) instead of 'I'm bad' (Young 1988) can help to focus their attention on changing their behaviour instead of damning themselves for it.

Badness is an EVALUATION that can be made of adverse events in the non-ego domain. Here you can help your clients to construct a continuum of badness from 0 per cent (e.g. a sock with a hole in it) to 100 per cent (e.g. nuclear annihilation) in order to place their present difficulties (e.g. end of a relationship, loss of a job) within a broader perspective. For those clients who find humour helpful, you can use the Johnny Carson technique to similar effect: 'How bad is it, Johnny?'

B–C thinking

See A–C THINKING.

begging the question

This involves assuming something to be true which, as yet, remains to be proved. For example, a client might say, 'I didn't stand up to that bully as a real man would have done, so I'm not a real man.' What is at issue here is what constitutes a 'real' man. Can a 'real' man still be a 'real' man if he does not stand up to bullies? What qualities make the client 'a poor excuse for a man'? By seeking to clarify such issues, you are asking the client if he really has proved his case or is the question still begging? Clients beg the question when they use self-depreciatory terms such as 'useless', 'repulsive' or 'no good' and a similar process of clarification can be initiated by you.

best friend argument

When a client condemns herself as 'worthless' for making mistakes, would she condemn her best friend in the same way if he made mistakes? The usual reply is 'No'. (If the client did condemn her best friend, you can explore the effect this might have on him and the relationship.) Why is she compassionate towards her best friend, but harsh on herself? The client is operating a double standard and it is important to tease out the beliefs underlying this double standard. For example, the client might be a perfectionist who believes she must not fall below her very high standards while her best friend 'is not in my league and therefore his mistakes are understandable and forgivable'. The client might see herself as unique (i.e. infallible) while viewing her best friend as part of the 'common (i.e. fallible) people'. If this is the case, how does she explain making mistakes? Making mistakes indelibly stamps her as a fallible (imperfect) human being, just like her best friend.

betrayal

'You've stabbed me in the back' is a common expression of betrayal, usually accompanied by anger and hurt. The person betrayed believes she is totally undeserving of such disloyal behaviour (e.g. her partner remains neutral during a dispute she has with a neighbour instead of supporting her or he contradicts her viewpoint when she is discussing events with others instead of agreeing with her). When a person puts her trust in another (e.g. 'Remember, I left my marriage to be with you'), there is often an unrealistic expectation that this trust should be honoured indefinitely and transcend changing circumstances or relationship difficulties. Also, when rigid expectations are held (e.g. 'You must never let me down'), a minor breach of trust (e.g. telling a white lie) is often transformed into an act of betrayal (e.g. 'Your lies have destroyed my faith in you').

From this viewpoint, broken promises spell betrayal rather than a realistic consideration of the difficulties the other person has in trying to meet her wishes some, most or all of the time. Realistic expectations of others' behaviour allow for the possibility of trust being renewed if promises are broken (e.g. an act of infidelity) rather than seeing betrayal as something the individual can never recover from or believing that everyone has to be kept at arm's length from now on.

blame

Blame involves not only finding faults with oneself or others but also denigrating oneself or others for these faults (e.g. 'I'm to blame for not getting the report in on time and therefore I'm incompetent'). Encouraging your clients to take responsibility for their problems can appear to them as if you are blaming them for having these problems (see EMOTIONAL RESPONSIBILITY). This erroneous assumption can be dealt with by distinguishing between responsibility and blame: responsibility is acknowledging what is realistically within a person's control (e.g. 'My angry outbursts when things don't go my way') without self-condemnation while blame is acknowledging what is within a person's control but accompanied by self-condemnation (e.g. 'I'm pathetic for having these temper tantrums').

Self-condemnation makes the burden of responsibility heavier to bear and adds nothing constructive to the process of problem-solving or learning from mistakes. If some clients insist on using the word 'blame', help them to separate situational blame (e.g. spilling a glass of wine over someone's dress) from self-blame (e.g. 'I'm a clumsy idiot') and take responsibility for the former (e.g. paying to have the dress cleaned) and refrain from the latter.

blow-up technique

This procedure involves asking your client to imagine future adverse events and then blowing them out of all proportion to what might realistically happen. For example, a client who believes that making a mistake at work will have dire consequences for the company is presented with a picture of the company closing down, hundreds unemployed, whole industries disappearing, the country grinding to a halt and a global recession unleashed. McMullin argues that 'to continue to embrace them [irrational beliefs], most clients keep their irrationalities just within the bounds of acceptable logic' (1986: 218). Pushing the client's irrational belief to its logical and absurd conclusion helps to undermine the belief and keep the client's worries within a realistic perspective (see COGNITIVE PARADOX).

boredom

Boredom usually involves not knowing how to make productive use of one's time; the person becomes lethargic or irritable at the lack of stimulation in his life. Is boredom inherent in a situation or the attitudes that an individual brings to the situation? For example, if you complain that one or two of your clients are 'really boring' because they never stop moaning about everything, what steps are you taking to try to make therapy more interesting for both of you, or are you just praying for the end of the session?

Even if a person finds it difficult to find any interest in a proposed activity, still undertaking it teaches him that he can tolerate intense boredom in order to reach a specific goal and, additionally, there is no reason why he should be exempt from experiencing such boredom. Learning to tolerate and deal constructively with boredom (e.g. reading a book while stuck in a long traffic jam) reminds us that boredom is a state of mind rather than a state that is imposed upon us by a situation.

brain thinking vs. gut thinking (Maultsby 1975)

'Brain thinkers accurately realize that it is their thoughts that cause their feelings; gut thinkers believe that feelings are experiences that just happen or are caused by events' (Grieger and Boyd 1980: 164). Gut thinkers often use 'I feel' statements when they really mean 'I believe' such as 'I feel a failure, therefore I am a failure'. By inserting 'I feel . . .' into the sentence, the person assumes that his feelings are facts when it is the person's beliefs that largely determine his feelings – 'I believe that I'm a failure, therefore I feel like a failure. That's why I'm depressed.'

Genuine feelings (not thoughts masquerading as feelings) are never challenged but, instead, orientate your gut-thinking clients to the beliefs underpinning their disturbed feelings and encourage them to look for evidence to confirm or disconfirm these beliefs. In this way, gut thinkers become brain thinkers and realize that how they think largely determines how they feel and can now clearly distinguish between 'I feel' and 'I think' statements (see EMOTIONAL REASONING).

brainwashing

When a client says she has been 'brainwashed' by others (e.g. her partner) into believing she is 'stupid' or 'useless', brainwashing really means she has accepted uncritically the views of these others. Why has she not subjected their views to scrutiny in order to make up her own mind? If she was told that she was a giraffe, she would probably question the reality of that statement (i.e. she would not accept it uncritically).

Even if she agreed with others' opinions of her (e.g. 'I am stupid'), this could be considered as self-brainwashing. You would need to examine her evidence for and against this self-appraisal. For example, 'I must be stupid because I couldn't answer the question' vs. 'I can't see how I'm not stupid' – this is hardly a balanced argument and no wonder the client continues to see herself as 'stupid'. Brainwashing, from whatever source it comes, only occurs if the person allows her critical faculties to become dulled through infrequent use.

but-rebuttal

Clients' '"buts" may represent the greatest obstacle to effective action' (Burns 1981: 98). For example, every suggestion you make for tackling a client's problems is met with 'I see the sense in that but . . .' – the 'but' often means that the 'sense' will not be translated into action. In order to mobilize the client into carrying out his agreed tasks, each of his buts is answered with your rebuttals. For example:

Client: I can see how the task will help me but I don't think I'll have the time to do it in the next week. I'm so very busy.

Therapist: If you won the National Lottery, would you find the time to go and collect the cheque?

Client: Of course. Who wouldn't? Okay, point taken. I'll attempt the homework but no promises.

Therapist: Would you attempt to go and collect the cheque or would you do it?

Client: I'd do it but the homework is not as appealing as picking up a fat cheque.

Therapist:	Is overcoming your problems appealing?
Client:	Yes, but not the effort involved.
Therapist:	How much effort have you put into avoiding dealing with your problems over the years?
Client:	A lot.
Therapist:	Will the effort to overcome your problems be more or less do you think?
Client:	I know it will be a lot less. Okay, no more buts. I'll do the homework.

Do not get into a 'battle of the buts' as this can turn into a power struggle. Simply point out to your clients that little, if any, therapeutic change is likely to occur if their 'buts' prevail in therapy. Your clients can use the but-rebuttal method on themselves as part of their developing role as a self-therapist.

caring

Some clients may disturb themselves over the problems of others and attribute this disturbance to the fact that 'I care – that's my problem'. Caring for others who are in need is a humane response but becoming disturbed about their plight usually indicates the person cares *too much*, i.e. she believes she has to suffer because she sees others suffering. For example, a person becomes depressed over her best friend's misfortunes because she believes 'It's terrible that life that can be so cruel to her'. The crucial questions to ask clients who care too much are these:

> Does your suffering help the victim? Are you more able to be of assistance because you have gone and upset yourself mightily over his problems? If so, how? Do you mean to tell me that you wouldn't know how to help someone unless you first worked yourself into a lather? . . . Isn't that a waste of time and energy?
>
> (Hauck 1974: 83)

Some clients have a black and white view of caring. They think that if they do not care 100 per cent for someone, then they are uncaring. Helping such clients to distinguish between uncaring, healthy caring (which takes into account the needs of oneself and others) and unhealthy over-caring (where 100 per cent of one's attention is focused on the other person and 0 per cent on oneself) can be very telling, i.e. they can now strike a balanced view of what constitutes caring.

cart-before-the-horse thinking

This occurs when clients want certain conditions to exist before they undertake a programme of change (e.g. 'I want to feel really confident about stopping smoking'). This client wants to reverse the usual order of human experience by expecting to feel confident before rather than after undertaking the task (increased confidence comes with repeated practice of the task). Similarly, clients may want certainty of success in advance of carrying out the task or to feel comfortable entering fear-provoking situations. Whether a person has succeeded in a particular endeavour comes with hindsight, not foresight; and if he wants to feel comfortable about staying in aversive situations, then he has to embrace discomfort now in order to feel comfortable later (Ellis 1985). Explain to your clients that if they want to be more confident, comfortable and certain, then they should stop putting the cart before the horse and realize that if they want the benefits of change, they first have to act unconfidently, accept uncertainty and court DISCOMFORT.

challenging, but not overwhelming

HOMEWORK assignments not only help your clients to develop both confidence and competence in tackling their problems, but also deepen their conviction in their new problem-solving outlook. However, if some clients take 'tiny steps' in the problem-solving process, this can convince them of the hopelessness of their situation (e.g. 'I'm getting nowhere') or reinforce their low frustration tolerance towards the hard work of change (e.g. 'I can't bear discomfort') while 'biting off more than one can chew' can convince other clients that any progress they have gained has been wiped out (e.g. 'I'm right back to square one').

Another approach to homework is to adopt the principle of challenging, but not overwhelming, i.e. tasks are sufficiently stimulating to promote productive change but not so daunting as to inhibit your clients from carrying them out. Negotiated homework tasks can be graded IC (insufficiently challenging), CO (challenging, but not overwhelming) or TC (too challenging) from the perspective of your client's current skills and progress.

cognition without ignition (Dryden 1985)

This refers to cognitive change without accompanying behavioural change. For example, a client says he is now self-accepting and there-fore will no longer reject himself on the basis of someone else's rejection of him. However, he still avoids asking women out despite his stated therapeutic goal of establishing a relationship. Is the client's new outlook of self-acceptance theoretical or actual? You

> . . . will not be confident that the patient has internalized a new philosophy until it is reflected in behavioral change. Patients in therapy are engaging in

verbal learning, and it is important to assure that their behavior in the real world matches their verbal behavior in session.

(Walen et al. 1992: 169)

So explain to your clients that developing a new attitude requires repeated practice of it – cognition with ignition.

cognitive paradox

This involves deliberately helping your clients to exaggerate rather than modify their self-defeating ideas. For example, you can point out to a client with approval needs (e.g. 'I must have his approval in order to be worthwhile') that she must work even harder to please others (e.g. 'It would be catastrophic to lose his approval, so you will need to devote every minute of every day to his welfare and comfort'). By feeding back your client's self-defeating ideas in an exaggerated form, you can encourage her to reappraise these ideas and the need for approval that drives them. Will she be more certain of his approval if she works harder to please him? What are the personal costs of seeking his approval? And what prevents her from engaging in self-approval irrespective of how others see her? Cognitive paradox is a humorous intervention with a serious purpose (see BLOW-UP TECHNIQUE).

commitment

When your client states his GOALS for change, this does not automatically mean he has committed himself to undertaking the hard work to reach these goals. You might find the client wants the gain without experiencing any real effort to attain it. In order to crystallize the issue of commitment at the outset of therapy, you might want to use this analogy:

> You want to complete the London marathon which is in nine months' time and you are currently unfit. In order to have a good chance of crossing the finishing line, you need to start training now on a regular basis to acquire the fitness and stamina needed for the race. Can you see the point I'm making with regard to overcoming your problems?

Grieger states that effecting change is 'a 24–hour-a-day, seven-day-a-week-thing' (1991: 60). While this may be an extreme position to take, it can be used as a yardstick by your clients to measure their own level of effort. Commitment also means you giving your professional best to each and every client rather than becoming bored, detached or cynical through listening 'to the same old problems'.

common sense

Clients often respond to the problem-solving LOGIC of cognitive-behaviour therapy (CBT) by saying it is 'all common sense'. By this, they usually mean that, since most people would give them the same advice as you have done, you are not telling them anything new and, therefore, you are not being helpful. Actually, the logic of CBT is developing an uncommon sense of each client's difficulties in acting on this 'common sense' – what prevents the client from putting into daily practice (emotional INSIGHT) his understanding of how to ameliorate his problems (intellectual insight)? For example, you have advised your client, just as his friends have done, that the way to overcome his fears is to face them. However, unlike his friends, you have uncovered, through detective work, the reasons why he blocks himself from taking effective action. Common sense cannot provide the detailed and idiosyncratic understanding necessary for a successful resolution of the client's problems.

confidence

Confidence is usually equated with success and SELF-ESTEEM, and confident people are often viewed as role models. However, a confident person is not necessarily a secure person: fear of failure and a perceived inability to cope with it if it does occur may be lurking somewhere in the person's mind. We believe that true confidence is not only taking risks, handling pressure and success without going off the rails, but also being secure in the knowledge that whatever setbacks occur, the person will always apply a problem-solving outlook to them. For example, a person may lose his mansion and end up in a bedsit but can still find some enjoyment and peace of mind in these straitened circumstances because he accepts the reality of these new circumstances. At the same time, he starts making plans to rebuild his life without assuming he has to get his mansion back in order to be happy again (any improvement would be welcomed). True confidence embraces both success and defeat.

control

Some clients choose goals which lie outside of their sphere of control (e.g. 'I want my boss to treat me better'). With this example, it is up to the client's boss to achieve her goals for her. Needless to say, if her boss does not make any positive changes in his behaviour towards her, then the client's difficulties will remain unresolved. You might need to go over this point a number of times before your client sees this distinction between what she can control and what she cannot (e.g. 'You can learn to act assertively towards your boss regarding his rude behaviour but it's his decision regarding changing it. By changing your behaviour *first*, you can attempt to influence, not control, his behaviour in a positive direction').

Clients who demand that they must be in control of themselves at all times (e.g. 'I must not show any weaknesses to my colleagues') continually reinforce their fear of losing control and the consequences for their self-image (e.g. 'I'll be seen as weak and pathetic'). When loss of control does occur, they usually become emotionally disturbed about it such as being angry, depressed and/or ashamed. Demanding self-control is the illusion of control. Real control involves not fearing losing it, being self-accepting (not self-condemning) when it does occur and constructively looking for ways to regain it. For example, a client who accepted that he blushed when he became the centre of attention ('It's part of me but I've been trying to suppress it for years') found that the duration, intensity and frequency of his blushing episodes decreased dramatically once he had internalized this 'control through acceptance' strategy.

coping vs. mastery

A coping model of PROBLEM-SOLVING is preferable to a mastery one. A coping model is based on reasonable problem management with room for improvement whereas a mastery model implies problem eradication. This latter model may reinforce some clients' perfectionist tendencies (e.g. 'I want to get on top of my performance anxiety so it never comes back') – coping is equated with mediocrity. However, if the problem is not mastered, then the client might believe she is back at square one (an example of all or nothing thinking). A coping model allows the client to switch her focus to other problems when the target problem is being adequately managed by her. Following a mastery model can mean the client gets bogged down in searching for complete success with one problem while neglecting to deal with other problems that also require her attention.

countertransference

This refers to the feelings and attitudes of the therapist towards the client. Weishaar observes 'that countertransference issues are regarded as signals for therapists to work on their own automatic thoughts and assumptions' (1993: 123). Leahy (2001) suggests that therapists should consider themselves as their 'own patient' in examining the countertransference. This examination starts with, for example, looking at your heart-sink reaction to certain clients (e.g. 'He says he is a hopeless case. I think he's right about that') or your feelings of anxiety as the time approaches for the arrival of the client (e.g. 'She just won't accept anything I say. She'll make me feel incompetent').

In the first example, you may have allowed yourself to be 'sucked into' the client's bleak outlook instead of remaining as an empathic but objective observer of his problems; in the second example, you can stop seeing yourself as incompetent if you do your best but put more of the responsibility on to the client for problem-solving suggestions – let her brain take some of the strain of therapy (CBT is supposed to be collaborative).

Leahy proposes 'that the countertransference is an excellent window into the interpersonal world of the patient' (2001: 6) as it can be used constructively to understand the impact the client may have on others in his life besides the therapist. For example, if you feel impatient and start speaking curtly to the client because 'he never stops moaning', your reaction may well reflect how others in his life react to him (e.g. the client says he gets fewer phone calls and visits these days). You are in a good position to give feedback to the client on how his behaviour influences you (which others in his life may avoid telling him) and what changes the client may wish to consider in an attempt to reverse his increasing social isolation (see TRANSFERENCE).

criticism

Receiving criticism may be unpleasant but it does not have to upset us unduly unless we allow it to. When a person says she feels angry and hurt by someone's criticism of her, this may be because (a) she believes the other person should not criticize her (see ANGER), and (b) she does not deserve to be criticized because, in her mind, she has done nothing wrong. We would argue that others are free to say what they want about us and whether it is justified or not is irrelevant. The important point for the client is to ask herself: is the criticism true or false?

If it is true, does she propose to take steps to modify certain aspects of her behaviour? If her critic attacks her (e.g. 'You're incompetent'), she can redirect his attention to a constructive evaluation of her performance (e.g. 'In what specific ways am I acting incompetently and what steps would you suggest I take to improve my performance?'). In this way, her critic has to put up or shut up! If the criticism is false, let the person know that he is barking up the wrong tree, allow him the right to be wrong and then she can return to the work he interrupted.

If a client says that constant criticism of him makes him feel 'useless' or 'a failure', ask him if he agrees with the criticism. As Eleanor Roosevelt pointed out: 'No one can make you feel inferior without your consent.' If he agrees that he is a failure, then the idea has not been put into his head by others (see BRAINWASHING) because it is already there. Elicit and examine the evidence for his self-appraisal as a 'failure' and help him to see that our behaviour may fail from time to time but never the entire person (Leahy 1996).

cutting to the chase

This means, in cognitive-behavioural terms, locating, as quickly as possible, the key cognitions that are maintaining your clients' emotional and behavioural problems. Therefore, you need to dissuade your clients from engaging in long-winded descriptions of their problems thereby often prolonging their distress in therapy. Instead, encourage your clients to put their finger on the nub of the problem by asking such questions as 'What are you most upset about?', 'What keeps this problem going?' or 'What prevents you from taking decisive action to deal with the problem?'

Cutting to the chase also involves developing, as early as possible in therapy, alternative ways of thinking and behaving that will have a positive impact on the problem. Encouraging your clients to look forward to what could be rather than focusing on what is or what has been, starts with enquiries such as 'What needs to change within you?', 'What would you need to say to yourself in order to stay in the situation rather than leave it?' or 'How would you like to see yourself instead of regarding yourself as incompetent?' Cutting to the chase may be too quick and too unsettling for some clients, but you can offer them the choice of a direct route to change or a circuitous one.

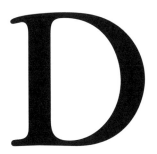

debate

Debate helps us to clarify our thinking about important issues and examine the arguments underpinning our viewpoint. The counselling room can be likened to a debating chamber where the client's maladaptive thoughts and beliefs (e.g. 'I must do everything perfectly') are discussed. Therapist-initiated debate promotes client self-debate. Hauck states that in all counselling

> . . . one task is more critical than any other. It is self-debate. Throughout your counselling it is practically always critical that you keep the client oriented toward questioning, challenging, and debating with himself over his irrational ideas.
>
> (1980a: 244)

Encourage your client to engage frequently in self-debate (ideally, on a daily basis) until his irrational ideas are attenuated and more realistic ideas emerge and are acted on (e.g. the client undertakes activities with the belief that 'doing things well' is the sensible alternative to his former self-inflicted agony of seeking perfection in all his endeavours).

decentring

This technique 'underlies all cognitive modification techniques [whereby] the patient is asked to stand away from his thought or interpretation and examine it in a realistic manner' (Blackburn and Davidson 1995: 78). Decentring allows the client to gain some objectivity in assessing the usefulness and validity of his disturbance-inducing thinking. Decentring provides the client with a choice between continuing to adhere to such thinking or modifying it and assessing the likely consequences that flow from each choice (the client may not realize he has a choice when caught up in the emotional heat of a particular situation). For example, a client who believes that 'displaying weakness is unforgivable' is asked to comment on a recent example where a respected work colleague showed a 'weakness'. The client says that his colleague's lapse was 'understandable and forgivable'. Decentring encourages the client to reflect on why he can forgive others but not himself for displaying weakness, and the hard time he gives himself when he does (see BEST FRIEND ARGUMENT).

decision-making

Decision-making can be a great struggle if your clients (and ourselves) adhere to some of the following indecision-inducing ideas:

1. I must be confident about the decision (because confidence implies a successful outcome).
2. I must feel comfortable about the decision (this is unlikely if the decision is not clear-cut and there are advantages in not making a decision).
3. I must be in control of the decision and its outcome (this can be true if you want a cup of coffee but not for decisions involving more complex factors like the reactions of others).
4. I must be certain that I have made the right decision (this comes with hindsight, not foresight).

Indecisiveness itself is based on a decision not to decide, but prolonged indecisiveness often means that a decision will be forced on your client by the inexorable march of events (e.g. not responding to letters requesting payment of rent arrears could lead to court action or eviction). Improved decision-making can start with collecting as much information as possible regarding the proposed decision, assessing both the source and quality of the information, setting a decision deadline, evaluating the pros and cons of each potential decision, and calculating the likelihood of a successful outcome for each decision (e.g. 'This one seems to have a 75 per cent chance of success'). When the decision has been made, further decisions are needed to sustain a successful outcome or ameliorate an unfavourable one. Decision-making only stops when we die.

demandingness

'Demandingness means believing that certain things must or must not happen; believing that certain conditions, such as success and approval, are *necessary'* (Wessler and Wessler, 1980: 42; original authors' emphasis). When demands are not met, emotional disturbance often results. For example, a person demands that he must get the promotion he has worked so hard for but becomes angry and hurt when he is passed over. Demandingness assumes that there is some absolute law of the universe that should implement the person's dictates and it is a personal calamity when this 'law' is not enforced. Demandingness does not recognize 'buts' in its inflexible outlook.

Desires, on the other hand, are realistic and flexible as they acknowledge there are no absolute laws of the universe that must fulfil our desires and are adaptable to changing circumstances if our goals are not realized. For example, 'I very much want that promotion but there is no reason why I must get what I want. If I don't get it, it is not the end of the world. I can still enjoy my job at my present level.' Unfulfilled desires are less likely to lead to emotional distress than unfulfilled demands. If some of your clients say they feel very upset when a particular goal has been blocked, determine if these clients have removed the 'but' from their goal statements and transformed, either implicitly or explicitly, desires into demands.

depreciation

Depreciation of self and/or others is a common feature of emotional disturbance such as DEPRESSION or ANGER (e.g. 'I'm worthless'; 'You're no good'). SELF-DEPRECIATION inhibits or restricts personal growth and change because the person is unforgiving of his failures, sees no value in himself and is continually self-critical. Depreciation of others is hardly likely to bring out the best in them or encourage constructive behaviour (e.g. a manager calls her subordinate 'a lazy, useless bastard' and wonders why he is sullen and continues to procrastinate over his workload). Depreciation turns people into objects of contempt: global negative ratings are assigned without any consideration of the FALLIBILITY and complexity of human nature.

Teach your clients to replace depreciation with acceptance of self and others as fallible (imperfect) human beings who are too complex to be rated in any way. Encourage them to focus on rating only aspects of the self (e.g. behaviours, traits) and seeking ways of changing counter-productive behaviours and self-defeating tendencies (e.g. 'I want to get my impulsiveness under control but I'm not inadequate because of my impulsiveness'). FORGIVENESS starts with accepting human fallibility and self-nurturing (i.e. treating yourself as you would somebody for whom you care) can now replace self-condemnation.

depression

Depression usually delivers a double blow: for example, loss of a job followed by loss of self-worth (e.g. 'I'm nothing without a job') or failure of a relationship equals personal failure (e.g. 'I'm useless without a partner'). As if the initial loss was not bad enough, the person seeks to add self-devaluation to it. Struggling under this burden, the person usually has a bleak view of his future prospects and a diminished capacity to effect meaningful change in his present circumstances.

Moderating the effects of this double blow can start with the client realizing that self-devaluation contributes nothing to a balanced understanding of why the loss occurred, what to learn from it and how to cope constructively with it. The loss does not reflect on the person's worth. The initial blow of the loss may be worsened by the client's insistence that the loss should not have occurred (e.g. 'My partner should have stayed with me'). Accepting the grim reality of the loss, and integrating it into his personal experience, helps the client to move on and view the future with some optimism.

de-skilling

You might believe that you have been de-skilled by your client's comments (e.g. 'You're not helping me at all'), your supervisor's (e.g. 'You're not using Socratic questioning enough') or a colleague's (e.g. 'It's a really tough case, so I'd better take this one'). With the above client, we would argue that you de-skill yourself because you are reluctant to tolerate the uncertainty of moving beyond your current repertoire of tried-and-tested clinical skills in order to acquire new ones to tackle your client's seemingly intractable problems.

Self-deskilling also occurs when you link specific criticisms of your performance with role depreciation (e.g. 'Her criticisms mean I'm a crap therapist') and compare like with unlike when you tell yourself that you should be as competent as a more experienced and qualified colleague. If you focus on the crucial question of 'How do I improve my clinical skills?' in an open-minded, determined and non-depreciatory way, you are much more likely to avoid the perils of de-skilling yourself.

digesting

By this we mean allowing information presented to be discussed and absorbed. Too often in our supervision of CBT students, we hear them asking clients standard questions (e.g. 'Why do you believe it's so terrible to fail?') in a mechanical way, clients parroting what they think are the right things to say (e.g. 'It isn't terrible, I suppose'), and then another question is asked by the therapist. There is little sense of therapist or client chewing over the other's comments or the therapist creating a milieu in which 'thinking things through' is given sufficient time and attention. Clients are hardly likely to internalize new PROBLEM-SOLVING attitudes if they pay lip service to them.

dilemma

This is a situation where a person is faced with a choice between two equally unsatisfactory alternatives. For example, if a person stays with her partner he will continue to abuse her, but if she leaves him, she imagines herself 'falling apart' as a result of living alone. A dilemma might develop into prolonged disturbance and indecision if the person insists that 'I must make the right decision' and envisages terrible consequences if she gets it wrong (see DECISION-MAKING).

The idea of equally unsatisfactory alternatives is not usually borne out by close scrutiny of them because of the way the person has constructed these alternatives (see 'NO WIN' SITUATION). For example, if the person could see herself coping reasonably well with living alone rather than 'falling apart', would she be more inclined to leave her partner? Also, making a choice is not irreversible or 'for all time', so if she chooses to stay with her partner she might change her mind two weeks' later or if living alone is proving seemingly intolerable, she can learn to make it more tolerable by joining local clubs or signing up with a dating agency.

Using a cost-benefit analysis can help her to clarify the short- and long-term advantages and disadvantages of each alternative. Staying in an abusive relationship will remain deeply unsatisfactory (stuck on one horn of the dilemma) while living alone may start off as unsatisfactory and fearful but eventually becomes satisfactory and fruitful (the other horn of the dilemma she frees herself from actually turns out to be an opportunity for personal growth and change). (See QUANDARY.)

discomfort

Change usually involves discomfort, sometimes considerable, and is a major reason why some clients terminate therapy prematurely. However, clients who seek to avoid discomfort often give themselves a double dose of it: berating themselves for not facing their problems and then these problems getting worse in the long term. Point out to your clients that by learning to endure the discomfort of the PROBLEM-SOLVING process – deliberately pushing themselves to feel uncomfortable – they will

> . . . finally find the work easy and comfortable. And even, at times, enjoyable. By courting and courting *dis*comfort, and by that hard route alone, you'll *later* become comfortable. Not right away – *later*.
> (Ellis 1985: 102; original author's italics)

The paradox of discomfort is this: avoid it to increase it; endure it to decrease it (see ENDURANCE).

'does it make it true?'

You can ask this question when a client becomes upset over another person's accusations (e.g. 'She said I was spiteful and selfish, not a nice person to know'). Encourage the client to step back from the accusations and carefully consider them: does she see herself as spiteful and selfish? Whose viewpoint, the client's or her accuser's, establishes the truth or falseness of the accusations?

Even if she agrees with the accusations – it does make it true in the client's eyes – you can point out that acting spitefully and selfishly is an aspect of herself, certainly not the whole story of herself; therefore, to conclude, on the basis of this aspect, that she is indeed 'not a nice person to know' is inaccurate as it constitutes OVERGENERALIZING and can lead to SELF-DEPRECIATION (e.g. 'If I'm not a nice person, then I must be truly horrible'). The client can learn, if she so chooses, to examine and change her spiteful and selfish behaviour within the compassionate context of SELF-ACCEPTANCE.

double standard technique (Burns 1989)

Why do some clients apply a rule more strictly to themselves than they do to others? For example, a mother condemns herself as bad for letting her child fall over and injure himself while she has words of sympathy, not condemnation, for a neighbour whose child suffered a similar misfortune. By uncovering the client's underlying belief, you can understand her reasons for having double standards (e.g. 'I must be a perfect mother to my children to make up for my failure in not holding the marriage together'). By encouraging the client to view herself in the same sympathetic way she would others in a similar predicament (e.g. 'I would tell my friends that it takes two, not one, to hold a marriage together'), double standards can be ditched and replaced with a single standard that is both helpful and realistic (Burns 1989).

effort

Insight can provide clients with understanding regarding the development and maintenance of their problems, but persistent effort brings about the changes they desire. While the majority of clients can see the logic of applying effort to problem-solving, some of them may baulk at actually doing so. With these clients you can point out that they have spent considerable *negative* effort in maintaining their problems (e.g. through seeking a series of quick fix solutions, grappling with the adverse effects of the problem) while *positive* effort will bring an amelioration in their emotional and behavioural problems. They cannot avoid effort in one way or another, but which type of effort is the more productive in the longer term? See LOW FRUSTRATION TOLERANCE.

emotional blackmail

Forward states that emotional blackmailers use FOG to ensnare their victims:

> Fear, Obligation and Guilt, the blackmailers' tools of the trade. They pump an engulfing FOG into their relationships, ensuring that we will feel afraid to cross them, obligated to give them their way and terribly guilty if we don't.
>
> (1997: 7)

In order for your clients to find their way out of the FOG, help them to discover what makes them vulnerable to emotional manipulation and bullying in the first place. For example, a client who had powerful approval needs, reluctantly agreed to engage in what she considered to be distasteful sexual activities because she feared her partner's disapproval if she did not (a fear which he played on). Once the client was able to give up her approval needs, embrace SELF-ACCEPTANCE and practise ASSERTIVENESS, she left the relationship to lead a more independent life. When the emotional blackmailer can no longer push the client's 'hot buttons', because she has disconnected the wiring, he is out of a job.

emotional correctness

This means being told how you should feel about a particular event. An example of emotional correctness on a large scale occurred after the death of the Princess of Wales in 1997. It seemed as if a majority of the nation was grief-stricken and not to feel this way was considered to be 'unfeeling', 'heartless', 'unpatriotic' or showing disrespect to her memory and all her good works. Some people who did not agree with the majority viewpoint eventually succumbed to it because of pressure or intimidation and, thereafter, professed to feel what they did not. How a person feels about an event is determined by how they evaluate that event, and some people who did not appraise her death as personally meaningful, said so and stood their ground.

On a smaller scale, when clients complain they are being made to feel 'what I don't feel', you can ask them why they are allowing themselves to be dictated to (e.g. 'Because if I'm not seen to be really upset over my nephew's drug habit, then I'm going to be called an "uncaring bitch" by everyone and sent to Coventry or something. I don't want that to happen'). Obviously the client has a choice between faking what she does not feel in order to avoid name-calling and being 'sent to Coventry' or expressing her true feelings and developing a coping plan to deal with these unpleasant consequences.

In combating emotional correctness, we are not arguing for rigorous emotional honesty at all times, but learning to discriminate between when it is important for the person to be true to her feelings and when it is not (see RATIONAL CORRECTNESS).

emotional reasoning

This occurs when clients confuse their feelings with facts, e.g. 'I feel a failure, therefore I am a failure' (see BRAIN THINKING VS. GUT THINKING). Emotional reasoning is not based on an objective analysis of a negative situation but on a distorted view of it (e.g. 'I feel I'll never be happy again, so it must be true'). Gilbert suggests that 'feelings are very unreliable sources of truth . . . so, as a general rule, if you are depressed, don't trust your feelings – especially if they are highly critical and hostile to you' (1997: 92). During times of emotional upset, help your clients to reactivate their rational reasoning to overrule their emotional reasoning and thereby put their problems into a more realistic and manageable perspective.

emotional responsibility

In REBT, this concept refers to our largely self-induced emotional reactions to life events based on how we evaluate these events. For example, a rigid outlook (e.g. 'I must have what I want') usually leads to disturbed feelings (e.g. anger) when goals are blocked, whereas a flexible outlook (e.g. 'I certainly want things but there is no reason why I *must* have them') usually leads to non-disturbed feelings (e.g. annoyance) when goals are blocked. Though some clients will be reluctant to accept emotional responsibility because they blame events or others for their emotional problems (see A–C THINKING), its eventual adoption can help them to achieve greater emotional control in the face of adverse events or others' unpleasant behaviour (e.g. 'Your insults used to hurt like hell but not now because I choose not to agree with them any longer').

Emotional responsibility acknowledges that events contribute (sometimes powerfully so) to our emotional responses but do not ultimately determine these responses (we do). Finally, emotional responsibility does not involve blaming the client for her problems (see BLAME) but underscores her personal ownership of them.

endurance

When you discuss the concept of endurance with your clients, many of them will probably believe you are advocating that they develop a stoical attitude to life (e.g. 'Just put up with everything in life. Great.'). What you will be actually advocating is endurance to realize a specific goal, not as an end in itself: 'You will need to put up with a great deal of discomfort and anxiety to overcome your agoraphobia and achieve your goal of going anywhere you like on your own.'

Endurance is particularly required for those who seek a QUICK FIX for their problems (see LOW FRUSTRATION TOLERANCE) instead of a lasting one (equation: the amount of effort put in = the durability of the result). The philosophy behind endurance is: 'I can stand it [whatever the *it* refers to], but I don't like it.' While your client is standing *it*, he is also learning ways of reducing the intensity, frequency and duration of the *it*, as in chronic pain, for example (see White 2001).

enlightened self-interest

This philosophy encourages us to put our own interests first and those of significant others a close second (first does not mean all of the time). Enlightened self-interest states the obvious truth that if we do not look after ourselves, who else is going to do it for us? For example, a person drives himself relentlessly and starts to suffer the effects of burnout: he becomes ineffective at work and bad-tempered at home. On the other hand, achieving a work–home balance prevents the person experiencing burnout thereby maintaining his effectiveness at work and avoiding disharmony at home.

Some clients may confuse enlightened self-interest with (a) selfishness, where the person puts his interests first all of the time and disregards the interests of others, and (b) selflessness, where the person disregards his own interests and places himself at the service of others (this may appear not so noble if the client sees himself as unworthy to pursue his own needs or craves the approval of others).

envy

Lazarus suggests that 'the core relational theme for envy is wanting what someone else has' (1999: 229). We distinguish between resentful and non-resentful envy. In resentful envy (which sometimes can become malicious) the person disparages the other person's good fortune or advantages and may seek to deprive him of them (e.g. 'That would wipe the smile off that greedy bastard's face if I destroyed his winning lottery ticket. All that money is wasted on him anyway'). At the same time, the person may try to convince herself that she is actually better off without the other person's advantages (e.g. 'With all that money, you wouldn't know who your real friends are'). People will frequently deny that they are envious because they do not want to be seen as mean-spirited or a 'loser'.

In non-resentful envy, the person honestly and openly expresses her desire for what the other person has but without denigrating him for it or attempting to deprive him of it. Additionally, she may solicit his advice on 'the secret of your success' (e.g. 'That's the third time you've won big on the lottery. How do you do it?') and refrain from trying to convince herself that she is somehow better off without the desired financial success. Probably the most important point to teach to your resentfully envious client is this: while another person may have the success she desires for herself, trying to improve her own position and fortune in life is more constructive than attempting to undermine, disparage or destroy someone else's.

errors

Making errors is not a sign of weakness or stupidity but an ineradicable part of human nature. Clients who complain that they should not have made mistakes are denying their human FALLIBILITY and wasting time on an issue that cannot be reversed (e.g. 'How do I make the mistake go away?'). If humans learn by TRIAL AND ERROR, these clients want to bypass this process and make an error-free progress through life. Paradoxically, what could they learn if they never made any mistakes to learn from? Errors are inevitable, so teach your client to accept himself for making mistakes and focus on learning from them – putting himself down only wastes time, holds back his progress in improving his performance and leaves the errors intact for longer. Failure does not reside in making mistakes but in doing nothing about them (Hauck 1980a).

esteem

The etymology of esteem shows it is derived from the Latin *aestimare* which means to 'fix the price of'. When clients report problems of low self-esteem they usually mean they see themselves as having low self-value. Fennell suggests that self-esteem 'refers to the overall opinion we have of ourselves, how we judge or evaluate ourselves, and the value we attach to ourselves as people' (1999: 6; see SELF-ACCEPTANCE). When clients say they want to increase their level of self-esteem they often look to external factors to bring this about (e.g. new partner or job, more friends). Externalizing one's self-worth can lead to the proposition: 'They think, therefore I am', e.g. 'They think I'm inferior, therefore I am.'

Basing self-esteem solely on external achievement, success or approval can leave the person highly vulnerable to future dips in or even collapse of his self-esteem if these external factors prove elusive or transient. In dealing with self-esteem, it is important to teach your clients that we all have equal intrinsic value as human beings, e.g. a newborn baby has not achieved anything in life yet (apart from being born) but is the baby of less value than an adult who has acquired material possessions and achieved some success in life? If your clients can accept and internalize this viewpoint (e.g. 'I am a person of value irrespective of what I achieve or what you think about me'), then striving for external achievement 'will be built on the solid foundation of a broadly positive view of yourself' (Fennell 1999: 6).

evaluation

In order to understand fully your clients' emotional reactions to events, focus on the evaluations they make of these events rather than on their descriptions, observations and inferences of them. For example, 'I might not get the job' (observation), 'I'm sure the interview panel thought I was a poor candidate' (inference), and 'If I don't get the job, I'll see myself as completely useless' (negative evaluation of self). By pinpointing the evaluative thinking that underpins clients' emotional disturbances, valuable therapy time is not wasted on discussing less important or peripheral cognitions (see CUTTING TO THE CHASE). When you have gained an understanding of the client's presenting problem, ascertained the distressing emotions connected with it and explained the role of negative evaluative thinking in emotional disturbance, you can then ask: 'What's your ET [evaluative thinking] in this situation?' Identifying, challenging and changing negative evaluative thinking leads to efficiency in problem-solving and promoting change.

evidence

Seeking evidence is a key method in CBT of testing the validity of clients' maladaptive thinking. For example, what is the evidence that supports the client's belief 'I never do anything right' and what is the evidence that disconfirms the belief? It is important for you to speak from the data (Beck et al. 1979), not from personal opinion (e.g. 'I'm sure you do some things right'). Examining data helps your clients to become better personal scientists so 'they can acquire correct information, use evidence logically, and construct sound, self-helping beliefs' (Walen et al. 1992: 4). However, problems can emerge with this process if you and your client disagree over what constitutes evidence:

Therapist: Getting to the session on time shows you do some things right, or at least one thing.
Client: Doing something right would be preventing my wife from leaving me.

Following this exchange, the focus would now be on collecting evidence to determine what things are within the client's control (e.g. getting to the session on time) and what are outside of it (e.g. preventing his wife leaving him). Another problem is when the client disqualifies objective evidence because of an underlying and unarticulated assumption (Gilbert 2000). For example, despite the accumulating evidence that the client does some things right, your probing reveals his underlying belief that 'I should always do everything right'. Again you would need to look at the evidential base for this belief.

Though your clients may become frustrated with your emphasis on evidence, learning to stand back from their upsetting thinking helps them not to confuse psychological events ('I think . . .') with empirical reality ('Just because I think it does not make it true').

exercise

Physical exercise develops strength and stamina. Mental exercise builds intellectual and emotional muscle. You might have some clients who are physically fit but mentally 'flabby', i.e. they do not practise challenging their self-defeating beliefs in order to develop and act on their new self-helping beliefs. For example, a client's mood dropped every time he reflected on being rejected by his girlfriend – 'She shouldn't have dumped me. I'm worthless without her.' In order to develop a robust outlook towards this problem, he continually and forcefully reminded himself that he was not immune from rejection, that he did not have to reject himself on the basis of her rejection, and he could learn to cope and be happy without her. By internalizing this outlook, he achieved greater emotional stability and looked forward to future relationships. When clients mention how often they go to the local gym, we ask them, 'How often do you spend time in your "mental gym"?'

exploitation

The type of exploitation we discuss here is the client's complicity in it. Clients may not like being exploited, complain loudly and bitterly about it but continue to let it occur because they believe they will eventually gain some benefit from it. For example, a client does all the running in a relationship because he hopes to hear his partner say she loves him, or an office junior who is treated like a dogsbody by her boss, puts up with it because she hopes to gain his approval.

You can ask these clients if the exploitation will stop when they get what they want or will it have to continue in order to keep what they have got? Also, these clients would probably not be complicit in their own exploitation if they had self-respect rather than a low opinion of themselves. If they were able to improve their SELF-ESTEEM, would they still believe they need the love or approval of others who treat them badly or take them for granted? In our experience, when clients say 'No' to this question, their complicity in their own exploitation usually stops and re-evaluation of their supposed needs begins (e.g. 'I don't need her love. Our relationship should be based on mutual love and respect, otherwise it's not worth having').

facts vs. inferences

Facts are verifiable while inferences are unproven assumptions. For example, a client infers that he is going to faint during a panic attack because he experiences light-headedness but, in fact, remains upright and conscious during the attack. Clients frequently see their inferences as facts – they do not seek any corroborative evidence. With the example of panic, feeling faint does not mean the person will faint: to test this out, he will need to drop his safety behaviours when he feels faint (e.g. holding on to someone or something) in order to discover that he does not faint – fainting is accompanied by a drop in blood pressure, whereas in panic, blood pressure rises. Clark points out that 'the only anxiety condition in which fainting actually occurs is blood injury phobia [where blood pressure drops]' (1989: 77).

Even if a client's inferences turn out to be correct (e.g. 'I'm right. She is going to leave me'), new and unrealistic inferences are frequently added to the facts (e.g. 'I'll never be able to cope living alone. I'll never be happy again'). How can the client foretell his future with such unerring accuracy? These are not facts about his future but projections based on his current depressive feelings and bleak outlook. It is important that you do not slip into offering your own inferences in order to try to improve the client's mood (e.g. 'You'll find another partner pretty quickly'). Instead, negotiate HOMEWORK tasks that help the client to determine if he can gain some accomplishment and pleasure from living alone rather than acting in ways that support his depressive thinking (e.g. sitting in his chair all day). By evaluating the information collected from the homework tasks, the client can see that living alone may be a struggle for him but one that he can cope with because his distorted, negative inferences have been shown to be invalid (see EVIDENCE).

failure

Hauck (1981) states that one of our most common fears is fear of failure. Yet Gilbert suggests that 'the secret of success is the ability to fail' (1997: 251). We would add: 'and not to be excessively upset by it and learning from the failure'. Time and energy are wasted when we attack ourselves for our failures because it implies we should be immune from them. Failure is an indelible part of human existence and our task should be to learn from our mistakes in order to make fewer of them. When your clients make mistakes or have setbacks, congratulate them on their success because they know what not to do next time. This is what progress is all about.

It is useful to help clients distinguish between 'failure' and 'failing'. The former can be seen as the end of a process (e.g. 'I tried two hundred different ways to do it, but I ultimately failed') while the latter can be seen as steps in the process (e.g. 'I tried one hundred and ninety nine times before succeeding on the two hundredth attempt'). This distinction can be expressed in diagrammatic form:

fffffffffffffffffffffffffffffffff $\rightarrow$ failure
fffffffffffffffffffffffffffffffffff $\rightarrow$ success
(f = failings)

Remember that a series of failings (e.g. not getting a number of jobs) does not have to result in failure (e.g. the person eventually gets a job).

fairness

Most people would probably agree that life is unfair but some expect this not to apply to them, e.g. 'I know life is unfair but it really is in this case because I was accused of something I didn't do'. The implication in this example is that the unfairness should not have happened because the person is innocent of the charges made against him. Some higher body or ruling force in the universe should have prevented this particular unfairness from occurring or should right this wrong immediately. While the individual, in this case, will have to fight to clear his name, this fight can be made even more difficult if the person is consumed by the unfairness of it all and slides into self-pity. Life will seem even more unfair at this point than it objectively is because of the person's reluctance to come to terms with the reality of events.

We would say that life should be unfair because that is the empirical, daily reality and therefore we will experience some measure of unfairness in our life. When events go in our favour, do we complain about this (e.g. 'Life shouldn't be fair to me')? Also, what is fair to us may not be to someone else (e.g. 'Why did he get the promotion instead of me?') thereby emphasizing the relative nature of fairness. Keeping an inventory of fairness vs. unfairness in our life may help to remind us of the simple truth that you 'win some, lose some' (see FALLACY).

'fairy godmother' thinking

This refers to the idea that you have somebody 'up there' looking after your interests and that, ultimately, everything will turn out for the best. While it might be comforting for the client to believe in imaginary beings, it is also prudent for her to keep her eyes focused on 'down here' instead of 'up there', i.e. the client takes responsibility for her own life and, through constructive problem-solving, things may well turn out for the best (though not all of the time). In this way, the client becomes her own benefactress.

fallacy

Some fallacies often encountered in therapy are listed by Freeman and Fusco (2000: 39):

1. Fallacy of change (e.g. 'You should change your behaviour because I say so').
2. Fallacy of ignoring (e.g. 'If I ignore it, then it will go away').
3. Fallacy of fairness (e.g. 'Life should be fair').
4. Fallacy of attachment (e.g. 'I can't live without a man').

If it is appropriate, you might play a quiz game in which you examine collaboratively the evidence to support a particular fallacy like attachment (e.g. the client has lived quite happily without a man for periods of her life) and then ask the client: 'Fact or fallacy?' Fallacies are based on faulty information processing, while arriving at facts means the whole picture has been carefully and objectively studied.

fallibility

To be human is to be fallible (imperfect). Clients usually agree with this statement then condemn themselves for having weaknesses, making mistakes or falling below their standards, e.g. 'I know I'm fallible but I shouldn't have made that mistake'. In other words, fallibility should be negotiable such as 'I don't mind being fallible some of the time but not when I'm making important presentations'. People with perfectionist attitudes do not like to acknowledge their fallibility as this is equated with mediocrity by them and removes their sense of being special or unique (see PERFECTIONISM).

Acknowledging our fallibility is an act of liberation because it allows us to push our egos out of the way and thereby makes us less likely to engage in self-condemnation when things go wrong. We can learn to improve our good qualities and strive to minimize our negative qualities. Accepting our fallibility is not self-resignation: learning from our mistakes in life is one way to help us to become less fallible and more efficient in achieving our goals. When clients sometimes announce that they have not carried out their homework assignments because they are fallible human beings, you can reply: 'You can be too fallible!' This means that it is not their intrinsic fallibility that prevents them from changing but rather a reluctance to engage in the hard work of change. They have the choice of how to manage their fallibility: effectively or ineffectively.

In a similar respect, some clients may use 'I'm fallible' arguments as an attempt to avoid taking responsibility for their actions or as a way of camouflaging their LOW FRUSTRATION TOLERANCE, as in the above example of homework non-compliance.

false dichotomy

This means dividing things into two opposing classes and not mentioning or considering other available alternatives, e.g. a client might say 'Either I'm likeable or unlikeable' overlooking the fact that people could also be neutral towards her. False dichotomous thinking implies rigidity of thought which is likely to lead to emotional problems (e.g. DEPRESSION) when the negative alternative is activated such as 'You're either a success in life or a failure and I'm one, big failure.' Clients might cling to either/or thinking because they believe it keeps life clear and simple or they lack the ability or information to consider other alternatives. For example, after teaching your client to weigh the evidence accurately, he is now able to see that learning from experience is more important than simply labelling himself as a 'success' or 'failure'. False dichotomies are another way of thinking that everything in life can be defined in black and white terms.

Be aware of your own false dichotomies such as believing that if clients are not collaborating with you on problem-solving, then they are being resistant. Alternative explanations could be that you have not explained to them their role in therapy or they want a different kind of approach to the one you are offering.

fear

Most clients know that in order to overcome their fears, they have to face them. However, some clients believe they have to be calm and confident before they can face them and it is inconceivable to enter fearful situations while in a fearful state (see CART-BEFORE-THE-HORSE THINKING). This outlook can mean that amelioration of their anxiety will be protracted as they wait for the elusive calmness to arrive. Fear does not have to prevent us from doing something that may appear dangerous or frightening but it can provide us with a rationalization for not doing so (Hauck 1980a). For example, a client might say, 'How can I possibly enter a lift when I'm feeling so anxious?' Subjective distress does not necessarily mean there is an objective danger or threat – in this regard, FEAR can be spelled out as 'false evidence appearing real'. Another rationale for handling fear while in a fearful state is that skills learnt while in a calm state or safe situation may not be recalled in a frightening situation (Beck et al. 1985a).

'feeling strange'

Clients frequently complain of feeling 'strange' or 'unnatural' as they work towards attenuating their long-standing maladaptive beliefs and strengthening their emerging adaptive beliefs. This conflict between old and new ways of thinking, feeling and behaving is called cognitive-emotive dissonance (Grieger and Boyd 1980). An example of cognitive-emotive dissonance is the 'I won't be me' syndrome (e.g. 'I'll lose my sense of who I am'). Clients might terminate therapy prematurely to feel 'natural' again. Explain to your clients that this dissonant state is a usual part of the change process and it will eventually pass (old habits may now seem unfamiliar). In other words: 'If it ain't strange, it ain't change!'

flexibility

Changing circumstances require adaptive responses from us. Research shows that people with good coping skills have learnt to think and act flexibly in the face of adverse events (Kleinke 1991). For example, a person who refuses to accept that he has lost his job (a) is not going to get it back, (b) may precipitate a period of depression and withdrawal, and (c) will delay looking for another job (possibly for a considerable period). On the other hand, a person who accepts the grim reality of job loss will avoid these negative consequences and embark on finding another job with reasonable haste.

When the going gets tough, Dryden and Gordon (1994) suggest there are two kinds of thinking open to us: adaptive, tough-minded, PROBLEM-SOLVING thinking (e.g. 'The shit has hit the fan. I'll clean the fan') and unadaptive, crumble-minded, making-the-going-even-tougher thinking (e.g. 'The shit has hit the fan. Oh God! What am I to do? Can't it be yesterday again? This shouldn't be happening'). In essence, flexible thinking aids your problem-solving efforts and engenders a sense of control, while inflexible thinking perpetuates your problems and the feeling of being out of CONTROL.

force and energy (Ellis 1979)

Clients may believe intellectually in their new beliefs (e.g. 'I would like but don't need the approval of others') but not emotionally as the old beliefs remain more persuasive (e.g. 'I feel in my gut that I do need the approval of others'). Not believing something emotionally means a lack of conviction in it. In order to gain this conviction, clients can use force and energy in expressing their new beliefs, e.g. a client now speaks up in every group she attends and powerfully reminds herself: 'If I say something considered stupid, too bad! I'm not stupid because I might say something stupid.' To get this point across, ask your clients to verbalize their new beliefs in a weak and insipid manner and then verbalize the same beliefs in a powerful and forceful manner (you may need to model this contrast in vocal delivery for some of your clients). A HOMEWORK task can be devised whereby clients compare the effects of using, and then not using, force and energy to tackle a particular problem.

Force and energy are to be used by clients when they have intellectual insight into their new and adaptive beliefs, i.e. they understand these beliefs in their head but do not yet believe them in their heart (see INSIGHT). If they have not gained intellectual insight into their new beliefs, then force and energy will be wasted (e.g. 'I've really tried to convince myself that I'm OK as a person, but it doesn't work. I'm not OK as a person – that's what I really think').

forgiveness

Forgiveness of self and/or others can be a very difficult issue to tackle. Self-forgiveness can occur if the person seeks to understand his behaviour within a compassionate context (e.g. 'I fell asleep at the wheel and caused a crash which killed my best friend. I was on my way home, driving through the night, because my mother was ill') instead of a condemnatory one (e.g. 'I'm wicked for what I did'). No human being is exempt from behaving badly, making mistakes or causing tragic outcomes. Self-forgiveness is not opting out of personal responsibility (in the above example, the person might receive a prison sentence) or avoiding making amends in some way, such as apologizing to the victim's family. Self-forgiveness does not mean the person will ever forget what he did.

Understanding the dynamics of self-forgiveness does not automatically transfer to forgiving others. The client may have been, for example, sexually abused by her father while her mother failed to intervene to stop it. Greater understanding of her parents' behaviour may lead to partial forgiveness (e.g. 'I can forgive her but not him'). As Kennerley points out:

> Forgiveness is not 'all or nothing' – it does not have to be absolute . . . as far as forgiveness is concerned, a most important step is forgiving yourself for having been abused. It is not *necessary* to forgive your abuser(s) or the person(s) who did not protect you. You might, or might not, reach an attitude of forgiveness, but you can still make peace with your past and move on
>
> (2000: 156; original author's italics)

free speech

Most people will probably say they are in favour of free speech but, when emotionally disturbed, some will want to restrict or suppress it (e.g. 'You shouldn't speak to me like that. Keep your bloody mouth shut!'). When emotionally disturbed, a person is a poor defender of free speech. Removing the disturbance and restoring the person's commitment to free speech starts with him understanding that tolerating others' opinions does not mean he has to like or agree with these opinions.

The old saying that 'sticks and stones may break my bones, but words will never hurt me' does not apply in the above example as the person is deeply hurt and angry by the 'words'. Why this is so focuses on eliciting the person's MEANING he attaches to these words (e.g. 'She said she couldn't stand the sight of me any longer. This means I'm some kind of repulsive, flesh-crawling freak. I must have made her sick being in bed with me'). Free speech is his partner's right, but he can also 'speak out' against his self-denigration by examining the evidential basis for it and thereby arriving at more accepting self-judgements (e.g. 'She can't stand the sight of me, but I can accept me, warts and all').

free will

In the debate on free will vs. determinism, CBT opts for constrained free will, i.e. we are able to think, feel and act with a certain degree of freedom. Clients frequently believe that they are at the mercy of all-powerful forces and, therefore, are unable to exert any control over or influence on their lives (e.g. 'I can never shake off the shame of failure'). In this example, the person believes that his 'failure' will act as a lifelong ball and chain. Can the future be so reliably predicted on present circumstances or can the person see that he has the ability to choose that tomorrow can be better than today if he thinks and acts differently about his 'failure'? The late and distinguished philosopher Isaiah Berlin stated that

> Action is choice; choice is free commitment to this or that way of behaving, living, and so on; the possibilities are never fewer than two: to do or not to do; be or not to be. Hence, to attribute conduct to the unalterable laws of nature is to misdescribe reality: it is not true to experience, verifiably false . . . it is always possible, though sometimes painful, to ask myself what it is that I really believe, want, value, what it is that I am doing, living for; and having answered as well as I am able, to continue to act in a given fashion or alter my behaviour
>
> (1998: 96)

You can point out to your clients that they make a multitude of choices every day (e.g. what to wear or eat, who to see, whether to come to therapy) and that coming to therapy implies that they do believe, however tentatively, that change is possible rather than their future is fated. With the above example, the client can hang on to the 'disgrace of failure' for the rest of his life or see failure as part of the learning experience of a fallible and self-accepting human being.

frustration

Emotional disturbance is not the inevitable consequence of experiencing frustration. Frustration 'is the condition of wanting something and not getting it, or not wanting something and having it forced on you' (Hauck 1980b: 55); for example, wanting a pay rise but not getting it, or next-door neighbours playing loud music and preventing you from having an early night. Frustration only becomes disturbance (e.g. anger, depression, hurt) when the person's preferences (e.g. 'Blast! I didn't want to get stuck in this queue') are transformed into commands and dictates (e.g. 'I damn well shouldn't have to put with this crap!'). In this example, the person seems to be advancing a narcissistic and rigid rule that he should be exempt from the discontents and inconveniences of daily living. It is useful to remind clients that frustration is inevitable; disturbance about it is not.

'fuck it!' philosophy

The cumulative effects of adverse events, negative feelings or interpersonal strife can lead some clients to declare 'Fuck it!', i.e. this declaration gives them permission to engage in or return to abusing drink or drugs. While there is nothing inherently wrong with saying 'Fuck it!' and indulging ourselves in some way from time to time to ease the pressures of life, it is important that this behaviour takes place within the context of self-discipline. This means that the period of self-indulgence does not involve harming ourselves or others, exacerbating existing problems, destabilizing our life or functioning, or undermining our longer-term goals. Saying 'Fuck it!' in the absence of self-discipline is unlikely to fulfil these conditions. When clients say that 'getting wrecked helps me to forget the shit in my life', I (MN) have suggested that learning and practising constructive coping skills will 'help shift the shit out of your life instead of leaving it there. "Fuck it" can then mean the resolve to try something different.'

generalization of learning

Once your client has learnt something in one context, this learning does not automatically generalize to other contexts – the client (or you) cannot assume a 'snowball effect' (Frisch 1992). Teach the client to deliberately generalize his learning from tackling present difficulties (e.g. anxious in social situations) to other related problem areas (e.g. anxious when giving presentations to colleagues). In this way, spreading the effects of change is undertaken in a methodical way instead of being left to chance or hope.

getting better

Your clients might tell you that they are feeling better but this does not automatically mean they are getting better (Ellis 1972). Feeling better can occur because you have, among other things, shown clients warmth and support, taught them to relax and provided them with reassurance, but they are not getting better because their distress-inducing beliefs (e.g. 'I can't survive without a partner in my life') remain unexamined and intact. When adaptive beliefs have been developed and acted upon (e.g. 'I can survive without a partner which I'm proving to myself on a daily basis'), then you can say clients are getting better. Staying better would mean clients maintaining their treatment gains on a lifelong basis (see Ellis 2001).

global thinking

Global thinking blows problems out of proportion as well as being inaccurate (e.g. 'I always do everything wrong and she always does everything right'). Such sweeping statements do not take account of exceptions to them (e.g. times when the client does things right and the other person does things wrong). Specificity and contradictory evidence helps to combat global thinking:

Client: I never do the homework. I'm useless.
Therapist: You've done homework on two occasions. How does that square with your idea that you never do homework?
Client: So I did it twice. What does that prove?
Therapist: It proves that on two occasions you did not consider yourself to be useless. How did you see yourself on those two occasions?
Client: Maybe not so useless, like I used to be.
Therapist: So how might looking at the facts of each situation be more helpful to you than relying on these sweeping statements like 'I'm useless'?
Client: Help me think straight again I suppose.

Putting events into a realistic perspective by focusing on accuracy helps clients to correct their faulty information processing which produces such cognitive distortions as global thinking (Beck et al. 1979). Additionally, it is important to tackle clients' negative global evaluations of themselves ('I'm useless' as in the above example), as these are equally inaccurate. Such evaluations can never define the complexity, changeability and totality of the SELF (this also applies to positive labels like 'I'm good'). For example, acting ineffectively sometimes is simply that; calling oneself 'useless' because of these behaviours is crudely reductionist ('I am my behaviour').

goals

Some clients might select goals that are either unrealistically ambitious or unrealistically unambitious. Looking at the drawbacks of shooting too high or too low forms part of the process of goal negotiation. Shooting too high (e.g. 'I want to achieve 100 per cent success in everything I do') can mean that the client quickly becomes demoralized when she realizes her goal is unreachable. Also, selecting unachievable goals can be a way of not trying or avoiding risk-taking because the goals are so unreasonable. Shooting too low (e.g. 'I just want to scrape by on my performance appraisal') can deliver an outcome 'as inconsequential as the goal itself and often feels like a "hollow victory" with no sense of accomplishment' (Cormier and Cormier 1985: 224). Goal theory suggests that people will work harder and deliver a better performance if the goal is a challenging one (Butler and McManus 1998).

gradualism

Helping your clients to move slowly in tackling their problems can become counterproductive if they move *too* slowly because you might be conveying to them that change can be achieved in a comfortable and painless way and thereby reinforcing their LOW FRUSTRATION TOLERANCE ideas (e.g. 'I can't stand discomfort or emotional pain'). Clients need to learn to tolerate DISCOMFORT so they can, for example, stay in feared situations during agoraphobic exposure until their anxiety diminishes and the urge to escape goes away (Zuercher-White 1999) or explore rather than try to avoid painful issues in order to revise faulty beliefs that such issues will be 'too painful to discuss' (Beck et al. 1990). Be careful that your policy of 'gradually does it' does not result in clients' problems being prolonged or strengthened (see CHALLENGING, BUT NOT OVERWHELMING).

gratification

Immediate gratification is pleasurable and not necessarily self-defeating, but it can become a habit that sabotages clients' longer-term goals. For example, a student engages in strenuous partygoing and excessive drinking while neglecting his studies. Failing his course, he reflects 'that I got things out of balance'. Teach your clients to aim for a balance between enjoying the pleasures of the present while planning and working constructively for the future. For those clients who believe, 'I want what I want and I want it now and damn the consequences', remind them of this: 'Wanting now, wailing later.'

Other clients might tell you that their philosophy is: 'Enjoy today because you might be dead tomorrow.' Point out to them that each tomorrow finds them alive, so they can postpone some of their pleasures because, in all probability, they still will be around to enjoy them. Finally, as philosophers have pointed out from Socrates onwards, pleasure is not the same as happiness. A life built on endless pleasure-seeking can become an empty and unhappy one.

grief

When grief-stricken individuals are told by well-meaning friends and relatives that 'time heals', this false assumption can complicate the grieving process. For if grief is time-limited, when is the end-point? The person might become angry with herself because 'I haven't got over it yet. My friends keep on telling me it's about time. What's wrong with me?' At the urging of her friends, she pushes herself into socializing when she does not feel ready to do so and suppresses how she really feels. Fleming and Robinson state that it is important to help the bereaved challenge the FALLACY that time heals:

> This expectation implies that the bereaved need not do anything, that simply the passage of time will lead to resolution. Grief, however, is anything but passive. The survivor needs to be gently made aware that it is not the time you have to use that dictates the course of grief, but rather how you use the time you have. In reality, one does not 'get over' (i.e., forget) the death of a loved one, but, instead, one learns to 'live with' the death of a loved one (i.e., to integrate the death and the life of the loved one into one's personal construct system).
>
> (1991: 148)

'Using the time you have' can be focused constructively on Worden's (1982) 'four tasks of mourning' and provides the conceptual framework within which grief work can be undertaken (Gantz et al. 1992). These four tasks are:

1. Accepting the reality of the loss.
2. Working through the pain of loss.
3. Adjusting to an environment in which the deceased is missing.
4. Withdrawing emotional energy from the deceased and reinvesting it in other relationships.

grin and bear it

Some clients might say that they work in jobs where they have to 'grin and bear it' (e.g. dealing with the public) which is making them 'stressed out' because they want to tell some people exactly want they think of them but, instead, are expected to say, 'Have a nice day.' Mann (1999) calls this the HAND or 'Have a Nice Day' culture where we fake what we do not feel and hide what we really do feel. However, given the fact that displaying synthetic emotions and suppressing genuine ones are part of the job clients have chosen to do, the obvious task is how to cope with such job requirements. One way is to give up internal demands which are increasing stress levels (e.g. 'She shouldn't be rude to me when I'm trying to apologize for the product being damaged'; 'He shouldn't be angry with me. It's not my bloody fault the queue is held up!').

From this perspective, the customer should be trying to understand the client's predicament instead of the other way round! The client can acknowledge that customers have a wide variety of reactions in dealing with their own frustrations and thereby avoid giving herself problems about their problems (e.g. becoming angry because a customer is rude).

In this way, the client reduces her own stress levels and seeks constructive ways to defuse a fraught situation (e.g. 'I'm sorry the queue is held up. I'll try to find out what is going on'). With this new attitude, 'grim and unbearable' is replaced by the resilience implied in 'grin and bear it' (see LOW FRUSTRATION TOLERANCE).

guilt

Guilt often involves clients assuming too much responsibility for events or the actions of others. This excessive sense of responsibility can stem from what we call the 'omni outlook': 'I should have known my daughter was taking drugs' (omniscient); 'I should have had the power to stop her taking them' (omnipotent); 'I should have been there to stop her' (omnipresent); and 'I should have been able to deal with this situation' (omnicompetent). Because the client cannot hope to meet these impossible and godlike moral standards, she concludes that she is a thoroughly bad mother for letting her daughter take drugs.

Tackling the 'omni outlook' starts with reminding the client of her status as a fallible human being, not a deity, and reviewing the facts of the situation:

1. *Omniscience* – the client's knowledge of the signs and symptoms of drug use was non-existent at the time; therefore, all the conditions were in place for her *not* to know her daughter was taking drugs. Hindsight might bring wisdom but it cannot alter the original facts of the mother's ignorance.
2. *Omnipotence* – if she could control her daughter's behaviour, then the drug use would have stopped. The more she demands that she should be able to control her daughter's behaviour, the more likely she is to feel helpless in this situation. She can control her own behaviour but not her daughter's; however, she can seek to influence her daughter's behaviour.
3. *Omnipresence* – the client can only be in one place at a given time and often this is not the place where hindsight suggests she could have been. Only God is everywhere; humans are often in the wrong place at the wrong time.
4. *Omnicompetence* – attempting to deal effectively with any situation takes time and practice with no guarantees attached; instant expertise is not expected or success preordained.

Once the client has accepted that her knowledge, control of others, ability to be in the right place at the right time and competence are limited, then she can re-evaluate her degree of responsibility for events and plan a realistic course of action (e.g. seeking professional guidance from a local drugs agency, joining a parents' self-help group).

gullibility

'I can't help it. I'm just gullible' might be the reply of some clients as to why their problems keep recurring. Gullibility can be seen as a form of MENTAL LAZINESS, i.e. the client is letting other people's brains determine his fate (e.g. 'I got arrested. My mate told me to break into the shop and I did. He said there would be no trouble and I believed him') and he seems content to play a subordinate role in life. It is as if the client is afraid to think for himself, and lacks confidence in his own opinions; so non-thinking becomes a habit and a handicap. Thinking requires effort and energy but

> . . . the more you do it the easier it gets . . . And don't say you can't think. The fact that you had a suspicion that what you were told wasn't true means that you started a thought, even if you didn't take it very far.
>
> (Hauck 1988: 10)

If the client starts taking his thinking further, then he is likely to become less credulous and more careful in evaluating what others tell him.

'guru' thinking

This type of thinking assumes that someone whose ideas you respect must be right about everything and cannot be challenged; therefore, you adapt your thinking to the guru's pronouncements, e.g. 'He said my thinking is muddled. He must be right because his thinking never is.' As Storr observes: 'Belief in a guru, while it persists, entirely overrules rational judgement. Dedicated disciples are as impervious to reason as are infatuated lovers' (1997: 18).

Whether the person sees himself as a guru or you see him in that way, remember to look down, not up – then you will notice his feet of clay. No human is the fount of all wisdom and it is important to consider carefully what you are being told by the guru; in this way, you retain your own powers of reasoning rather than surrendering them. You might then find that the guru is adept at dispensing both original thinking and claptrap. The next time you are in the presence of a guru, remind yourself to stand on your own feet rather than sit at his.

hate

Some clients are so consumed by their hatred of others that they are often unaware of the highly corrosive effects it is having on them. For example, a client who was mugged – not very badly as he later admitted – spent many months determined to 'get even' by walking the streets at night carrying a knife and hoping to meet the muggers again. Meanwhile, his quality of life rapidly deteriorated, e.g. he lost his job, started drinking heavily and, after prolonged and frequent outbursts of anger, his wife initiated a temporary separation as he would not seek professional help. The point to make to such clients is that hatred and revenge often cause 'an enormous amount of suffering which [is] far in excess of the suffering they received at the hands of others' (Hauck 1980b: 89). After conducting a lengthy cost-benefit analysis of his hatred, the client was able to conclude: 'I mugged myself much more severely than they ever did.'

In self-hatred, the self is treated as the hated enemy (Gilbert 1997). The person may hate herself because of some perceived defect (e.g. big nose) or weakness (e.g. binge eating) or as a result of the actions of others (e.g. sexual abuse). Like hatred towards others, self-hatred has equally destructive effects (e.g. self-harming, depression, feelings of inferiority). If hatred is a form of self-poisoning, compassion towards oneself is its antidote (e.g. 'Why should I continue to hate myself for what others did to me?'). However, as Gilbert points out:

> You will need to be absolutely honest with yourself and decide whether or not you want hatred to live in you. Only when you decide that you do not, can you train yourself to become its master rather than allowing it to master you.

> (1997: 113)

Letting go of hatred towards self or others makes the person's world, both internally and externally, a better place to live in.

helplessness

Feelings of HOPELESSNESS and helplessness are usually found in depression. Helplessness is a state of mind, not an empirical fact. As Knaus observes:

> From a logical perspective, helplessness is an ungrounded conclusion based on a major assumption that there is nothing you can do to change. You can challenge that assumption through this straightforward question: where is the evidence that you will live life without the opportunity to exercise choice? If you can exercise choice, even the choice of declining to do anything to break out from a depression, you're not helpless.
>
> (1998: 139)

The fact that your client turns up for therapy militates against the idea of helplessness. Every little bit of effort attempted by the client chips away at the cognitive edifice of his helplessness and makes it more likely he will begin to experience some success (see HOPE).

high frustration tolerance

The prospect of change is usually more enticing than the hard work involved in realizing it. In order to ingrain new and adaptive habits of thinking and behaving, clients need to develop high frustration tolerance (HFT) to cope with the frustration, discomfort, uncertainty and strangeness associated with the change process. HFT can be summed up as: 'I can stand it, but I don't like it.' Your clients do not have to like 'it' (e.g. intense discomfort) but what will they gain if they stand it? Some clients might say 'I don't think I'll be able to develop HFT', but point out to these clients that, in fact, they already have a dysfunctional form of HFT – the ability to tolerate not only their original problems but also the additional problems that flow from them (e.g. anxiety plus social isolation). You can say to your clients: 'You have a self-defeating form of HFT which maintains the status quo. You can acquire a self-helping form of HFT which will help you to change the status quo and improve your life. The choice is yours.' Putting up with one's problems is usually harder than changing them (Ellis 1985; see LOW FRUSTRATION TOLERANCE).

hindsight

Hindsight can be very cruel if a person believes she should have thought or acted other than she did (e.g. 'I should have stopped my daughter going on that camping trip. She would still be alive today if I'd done that'). In other words, the person should have known at that time the tragedy that was to occur two days later. Unfortunately, foreknowledge was neither accessible to her nor was she capable of acquiring it, so how she thought and acted *at the time* was based on how she viewed the situation *at the time* (e.g. 'I don't mind you going camping with your friends. Just be careful and have a good time'). As Kubany says, clients with hindsight-biased thinking need help to 'realize that it is *impossible* for knowledge acquired after an event to guide preoutcome decision making' (1998: 134: original author's emphasis). Accepting this ineluctable truth can help the person to avoid experiencing a chronic grief reaction to the loss of her daughter.

homework

Homework is the arena where clients put learning into practice. As Beck et al. state: 'The patient is encouraged to view homework as an *integral, vital component* of treatment. Homework is not just an elective, adjunct procedure' (1979: 272; original authors' italics). Despite explaining the rationale for homework and dealing with clients' questions and/or reservations about it, some clients may be reluctant or refuse to engage in such assignments. In order to motivate these clients, you can ask them to assess the likely course of therapy with and without undertaking homework; or seek a compromise whereby they undertake homework one week but not the next and then review the findings. If they have children, are (were) they keen for them to do their homework? The usual answer is 'Yes', because they want(ed) their children to gain a good education and get on in life. CBT homework is about learning and self-development – why encourage for their children what they are now denying for themselves? (See DOUBLE STANDARD TECHNIQUE.)

hope

Jerome Frank has argued that one of the major curative factors of psychotherapy is that it engenders hope (Frank and Frank 1991). I have suggested (Dryden 1994a) that helping clients to see that they have been successful in dealing with past problems, and can therefore regard themselves as inspiring but realistic role models, can be a powerful way of engendering hope in them. It is important that you maintain an optimistic outlook that change can occur despite every suggestion you make being 'shot down' with a 'YES, BUT . . .' reply. Generating hope with clients who are depressed and feel hopeless about any positive change occurring in their lives may seem like a contradictory expectation, but as Schuyler suggests:

> . . . it is possible, I have found, for a depressed person to maintain simultaneously a pessimistic outlook on the future and an attitude of hope about the likelihood of the therapy to achieve a desired result.
>
> (Schuyler 1991: 16)

Persistently looking for a problem-solving breakthrough with intractable problems ('We're going to keep at it') is a way of keeping hope alive and often the most helpful element of therapy reported by clients who have eventually recovered (Beck et al. 1979).

Drawing up a problem list with the client makes seemingly overwhelming and limitless difficulties clear, specific, finite and manageable ('We are imposing order on chaos, bringing clarity to confusion'). As Fennell observes: 'This process of "problem-reduction" is crucial to the encouragement of hope, since it implies the possibility of control' (1989: 179).

hopelessness

Research has shown that hopelessness is the single best predictor of eventual suicide (Beck et al. 1985b; Greenberger 1992). Typical statements of hopelessness include 'I'll never get any better', 'I'd be better off dead' and 'I have nothing to look forward to'. Making inroads into hopelessness can start with some of the following points:

- The client is insisting that she finds a way forward right now rather than accepting that it may take time before she sees light at the end of the tunnel.
- Her hopelessness is a reflection of her depression, not an accurate picture of reality – when she feels better she is likely to find that hopelessness is not a permanent part of her future any more than it was a fixture in her past.
- If the client is sceptical that therapy can help her, would she like to apply the same scepticism to her belief that hopelessness is a valid response to events in her life (Leahy and Holland 2000)? It might turn out that therapy can help her by encouraging her to see that her sense of hopelessness is a very constricted and literally life-threatening way of viewing events.
- How does she know her family will be better off without her? All the evidence points in exactly the opposite direction: they would be

extremely distressed and unhappy if she killed herself. Is this what she means by them being better off without her?

- Similarly, if the client believes she will be better off dead, how is she going to prove this? How can she rectify the mistake if she is wrong? It is better to make rectifiable mistakes by staying alive and developing problem-solving options than make a decision which is irrevocable.
- Hopelessness and hope compete for supremacy during a suicidal crisis (Shneidman 1985) and it is by no means a foregone conclusion that the former will prevail over the latter. Even a small glimpse of hope chips away at the client's hopelessness beliefs.
- If her best friend felt hopeless and suicidal, would she agree with her friend's viewpoint or would she do her best to instil hope in her friend? All the arguments she would use to instil hope in her friend can be used on herself (see BEST FRIEND ARGUMENT): 'If your best friend's life is worth saving, then why not yours too?'

Beck et al. suggest that 'by introducing "cognitive dissonance", that is, demonstrating the inner contradictions in the belief system, we can open up this closed system [of thinking] to reason and to corrective information' (1979: 216–17). Rudd et al. suggest that during a suicidal crisis,

> . . . it is important to target the patient's *Source Hopelessness* in order to diffuse the immediate crisis. This is the precipitating event or circumstance that triggered the patient's suicidality. In other words, what is at the root of the patient's hopelessness during this crisis?
>
> (Rudd et al. 2001: 163; original authors' italics)

For example, a father's momentary inattention resulted in his young son being run over and killed by a car. He felt overwhelming guilt because he believed 'I killed my son and I'll never be able to forgive myself.' Examining the key issue of intentionality (i.e. did he deliberately distract his attention so his son could run out into the road and be killed?) helped him to see that it was 'a tragic accident that killed my son, not me' and that the slow process of self-forgiveness could begin (see HELPLESSNESS).

hostility (client)

Becoming defensive is understandable when you are under attack from hostile clients but is not therapeutically productive as both sides can become entrenched in their respective viewpoints. If you try to see the world through the client's eyes, you will probably understand the reasons for his behaviour (e.g. he believes that his problems were not taken seriously by the doctors he had seen and you will probably be the same). I (MN) once saw a client with a history of tranquillizer dependence who, during our first session, was extremely angry about the 'fucking uselessness' of all mental health professionals to wean her off the tranquillizers:

Client: You don't care about me. I'm just another headcase to you.
Michael: You're right about caring: I can hardly care about you when I don't know you yet. If I was to tell you that I cared for you, would you believe me?
Client: No, I bloody well wouldn't!
Michael: Good, so we're not going to have any dishonesty between us then.
Client: What good is that if you're going to give up on me like everyone else?
Michael: Yes, I might reach that point like others before me, but I will do my professional best to get you off these tablets and not reach that point. If I give you my best, will you give me yours in order to form a partnership to get these tranquillizers out of your life?
Client: OK, but I'm still very wary you don't mean what you say.
Michael: You're right to be very wary based on your previous experience, but are you willing to give me the benefit of the doubt for the next several weeks as a start?
Client: That seems reasonable.
Michael: Good. Let's get to work then.

Seeing some truth in the client's viewpoint rather than trying to defend myself helped to defuse her hostility and laid the basis for developing a THERAPEUTIC RELATIONSHIP. In the place of angry outbursts (which occasionally occurred), we agreed that frequent progress reviews would be more productive. Finally, behind her hostility was her vulnerability and despair – that no one cared about her problems and she would be a 'prisoner of tranquillizers' for the rest of her life – which I would not have detected if I had focused on 'How dare she talk like this to me?' thinking.

'how' vs. 'why' questions

'How' questions point forward while 'why' questions look back. For example, contrast 'How do I get rid of these panic attacks?' with 'Why did these panic attacks happen to me?' While the majority of clients probably want some understanding of the acquisition and development of their problems, dwelling on the 'why' can create the erroneous impression that finding the answer to it will bring about an improve-ment in their present functioning. The more important INSIGHT required is how clients' present problems are being maintained and how to modify or change these maintaining factors – the goals of CBT. In essence, 'why' is likely to keep clients trapped in rumination and inaction while 'how' allows them to step back from their problems and devise action plans for change.

hurt

When a person feels hurt she usually believes that she has been treated unfairly and is undeserving of such treatment. Withdrawing from the person(s) who has 'hurt' her (sulking) often occurs. For example, a person who did not get the promotion he thought he deserved, spent most of his time in his office, away from his colleagues, brooding on his 'betrayal' by the company he had worked so hard and loyally for. Clients frequently say their hurt is justified because they were criticized, rejected, disapproved of or betrayed by significant others, e.g. 'I shouldn't be treated like this. I listen to his day at work, so he should listen to mine'. However, others do not have to follow our 'shoulds' – they operate according to their own wishes and needs which may not always coincide with ours. Hurt is based on demands that others should reflect in their behaviour and outlook our notions of fairness, and life is awful when they do not do this.

Giving up hurt starts with accepting that others have a right to think and act in ways that are contrary to ours (e.g. 'He doesn't have to listen to my day at work, but it would be nice if he did'); acknowledging that while we may deserve not to be treated in a particular way, we do not *have* to get what we deserve in life; asserting our views regarding the perceived injustice instead of closing down channels of communication when we sulk; attempting to effect some of the changes we desire; and understanding that life is both fair and unfair, so we do not have to be too upset when we get our share of unfairness.

hypotheses

Some clients might object when you tell them that CBT treats their thoughts and beliefs as hypotheses rather than as facts (e.g. 'What I'm telling you is true!'). However, you are not there to judge a priori whether a client's statement (e.g. 'Everyone is against me') is true or false, but to encourage the client 'to regard his thoughts as a series of psychological events which consist of his own personal construction of reality and are not necessarily a true representation of reality' (Beck et al. 1979: 80). Hypothesis-testing allows clients to 'open up' their closed, problem-perpetuating system of thinking by gathering evidence-based data to generate alternative viewpoints with which to understand and tackle their problems. In this way, hypothesis-testing allows for the possibility of change, whereas 'facts' (e.g. 'I'm no good') seem immutable.

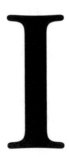

'I-can't-stand-it-itis'

See LOW FRUSTRATION TOLERANCE.

'I don't know'

You probably have heard this reply many times in therapy. Some clients say it so often that you may have difficulty in trying to suppress your irritation with this 'know nothingness' (some clients are embarrassed and/or irritated with their repeated 'don't knows'). Little, if any, progress will be made in the absence of client-generated data. Therefore, help clients to discover what they do know by, among other things, offering suggestions, engaging in imagery exercises, conducting behavioural experiments, encouraging clients to make guesses, suggesting the opposite of what might be the hypothesised thought or feeling (Beck 1995). In this dialogue, the therapist tries different ways to stimulate client introspection:

Therapist: You said you got very angry with your wife for coming home late and ruining the dinner you had prepared for her. What thoughts went through your mind to make you so angry?

Client: I don't know. I just got angry.

Therapist: Well, did you say to yourself something like 'It's okay. She couldn't help coming home late'? (Therapist suggests the opposite of what might be the client's expected response.)

Client: I don't know.

Therapist: Let's go back to the scene then: imagine you have spent several hours preparing the meal and arranging the room to create that special, romantic atmosphere and it's all for nothing because she comes home two hours late. What did you want to do at that point?

Client: (visibly tensing) I wanted to smash the house up, throw the dinner at the wall.

Therapist: And you would behave like that because . . . ?

> *Client:*   Because she takes me for granted. She knows I won't leave her no matter how she treats me. I despise myself for my weakness and hate her for her strength.
>
> *Therapist:*   Are those the reasons you were so angry? (Client nods.)

See each 'I don't know' response as an opportunity to increase your creativity and skill as a therapist by helping clients to bring information into their awareness that is currently outside of it.

'I don't know' can also be seen as a form of MENTAL LAZINESS, i.e. the client is attempting to get the therapist to do his thinking for him. You can time unobtrusively the latency period between asking a question and receiving the reply 'I don't know'. Is there any obvious effort on the client's part to process actively your questions? (Sometimes the reply is delivered the moment you have finished your question.) If there is no obvious effort, ask your client: 'If you don't give my questions due thought and consideration, how much progress are you likely to make in therapy?'

'I haven't the time'

This is a frequent reply when clients are asked if there are any obstacles to carrying out their agreed homework tasks. You can ask clients if they would be able to find the time to meet their favourite pop star, actor, author, etc. The usual reply is 'Yes'. Therefore, time is not the problem, but MOTIVATION. Uncovering the client's motivation-sapping ideas (e.g. 'I'm afraid that my family and friends won't like the new me') can help you to understand why she cannot find the time for homework. Conducting a cost-benefit analysis of tying personal change to the reactions of others can help the client to see that the eventual benefits (e.g. 'I'll be able to be my own person at long last') outweigh the probable costs (e.g. 'I know that a few of my friends will turn against me') and increase her motivation to undertake homework.

When clients say 'I haven't got the time', point out this paradox: they find the time to maintain their problems (e.g. a highly stressful lifestyle), but cannot find the time to tackle them.

'I won't be me'

See 'FEELING STRANGE'

ideals

How we would like to be and the reality we settle for has been described by Gilbert (2000) as the 'disappointment gap'. When a person falls below his ideals and becomes overly upset about having to settle for second-best in life, we would call this the 'disturbance gap'. The disturbance arises when demands the person makes on himself, others or the world are not realized, e.g. 'I absolutely should have been able to arrange my life in the way I've always wanted, but because this will never happen now, my life cannot be anything else but awful.'

Ideals represent distant points in our life and encourage us to strive to reach them, but introducing self-created imperatives (e.g. MUSTS, have to's, absolute shoulds) into this striving insists that possibilities become certainties. To paraphrase Oscar Wilde: we may be in the gutter but are looking at the stars. Maybe being closer to the stars than the gutter is the best that most of us can hope for.

identity

Seeing certain conditions or qualities as central to one's identity can create emotional problems when these conditions or qualities disappear from one's life. For example, a person who believed 'My work defines who I am' slumped into a depression when he lost his job: 'I've not only lost my job, but also my identity'; another person, who prided herself on her fitness and sleek body image, became despondent and angry when she put on weight and lost her fitness after a prolonged bout of illness – 'I'm not me any more'. Identity is much more complex than narrowing it down to a few features. Though some features will be more important than others, to make these features all-important – the central part of our identity – is to store up trouble for ourselves as the above examples show.

Kleinke points out that 'People who have a one-dimensional view of themselves are very limited. They don't have a broad foundation of personal resources to fall back on when facing difficult challenges' (1991: 208). Our identity can be based on the fact we are human and alive and what we do and achieve in life can never truly define us, so losses we experience (e.g. looks, partner, fame) do not involve a loss of identity. To become a good coper in life, develop your personal identity along many dimensions (Kleinke 1991) and thereby avoid the trap of putting all your eggs into one or two baskets.

indifference

A client might state her goal as indifference, e.g. 'I just want to say "who cares?" about the end of the relationship', when her real feelings are, for example, anger and hurt. If you agree to this goal of indifference, you will be helping the client to live a lie – pretending that she does not care when, in fact, she does. Living a lie will be very difficult, if not impossible, for her to sustain. The client might be reluctant to express her true feelings as she fears being overwhelmed by them. The client's fear can be allayed by helping her to distinguish between caring about the end of the relationship (e.g. 'I feel sad about it because it meant a lot to me, but over it is and I'd better move on') and caring *too* much about it (e.g. 'Why did it have to end? It meant everything to me. I can't go on without him'). If the client can see the sense in making this distinction, she will be more likely to give up indifference as a goal.

Indifference also means that if a client is faced with a choice between a positive and negative outcome (e.g. looking after his health or letting it deteriorate), it truly would not matter to him which outcome occurred. This is rarely the case in matters concerning the client's PERSONAL DOMAIN.

inference–evaluation distinction

In REBT, inferences are associated with emotional disturbance, but evaluations are central to it. A client says he is highly anxious about a forthcoming presentation he is going to make to his colleagues and supplies a string of inferences to explain how he feels: 'I'm going to trip over my words. They'll laugh at me. The presentation will go poorly. I'll be seen as the company idiot.' These inferences may be true or false but it is the evaluation of their possible truth (Walen et al. 1992) that largely determines how he feels about the presentation. Evaluating these inferences in a catastrophic way is the key determinant in producing his anxiety, e.g. 'If I screw up it will be truly awful. It will prove that I am an idiot.' Explain to your clients that emotionally-charged thinking ('hot cognitions') is usually evaluative rather than inferential in nature (see EVALUATION).

inferiority

When clients judge themselves to be inferior in some way, they are often making unfavourable comparisons with others, e.g. 'I'm inadequate because I'm tongue-tied and shy while she is charming, outgoing and articulate'. In this example, the client may have inferior social skills to the person she is comparing herself to, but that is all. Concluding that she is inferior as a person because of her social skills deficits is a wholly inaccurate and illogical judgement – there are no inferior or superior people, just people with different traits and skills. Therefore, her new conclusion could be: 'We are unequal in our social skills but equal as people.'

Sometimes clients will say that other people 'make me feel inferior'. For example, 'Some of my work colleagues say I'm fat, unfit, undisciplined, and smoke and drink too much. They make me feel like a slob.' As Eleanor Roosevelt remarked: 'No one can make you feel inferior without your consent.' The client agreed that he did give his 'consent' – 'I don't like what they say about me, but I suppose I do see myself as a slob.' The client's feelings of inferiority could be removed by accepting the way that he was, irrespective of how others saw him, and then deciding to make changes in his habits and lifestyle because he wanted to, not to make himself more acceptable to others.

insight

A crucial insight for clients to gain is the relationship between their thoughts, feelings and behaviours and the primacy of cognition in this relationship, e.g. 'Your thinking plays a powerful role in generating your anger when your wife ignores you' (see EMOTIONAL RESPONSIBILITY). However, the client might adhere to his own understanding of his problems, e.g. 'My wife makes me angry. End of story.' Instead of a 'competing insights' struggle for supremacy in therapy, facilitate the insight process by helping the client to see inconsistencies in his view of emotional causation:

Therapist: Now, your wife makes you angry when she ignores you. Right? (client nods). Now what would you need to say to yourself (tapping forehead) in order to feel happy, not angry, when she ignores you.

Client: Well, I suppose something like 'Good. I've got more time to do what I want.'

Therapist: What would you need to say in order to feel indifferent if she ignored you?

Client: I suppose 'I couldn't care less.'

Therapist: So how come you have thoughts accompanying those two feelings, but no thoughts when you're angry?

Client: (musing) Hmm. I suppose I do have them.

Therapist: Such as . . . ?

Client: (becoming agitated) Such as 'She shouldn't ignore me. What did she marry me for if she is going to ignore me? I don't ignore her. I hate to be treated like that.' (pause) Okay, the penny is dropping.

If the client had said that his wife caused all three of his emotional reactions, then it would be important to discover where in his life he does see the thought-feeling link and why it does not apply with his wife (e.g. 'I don't want to feel angry with her, so how can I have made myself angry?').

When clients have gained insight into the thought–feeling link and accepted its relevance to their problems, then the next insight for them to acquire is that insight alone is insufficient to promote therapeutic change. For example, ask them to imagine trying to change being right-handed to being left-handed simply by acknowledging that they are right-handed (Grieger and Boyd 1980). SKILLS-acquisition or internalizing a new outlook takes repeated and energetic practice.

Sometimes clients say about their newly acquired rational beliefs that 'I believe them intellectually but not emotionally'. This distinction between intellectual versus emotional insight is a FALSE DICHOTOMY: it is the degree of conviction in the new beliefs that clients are really referring to. As Walen et al. observe:

> 'Emotional insight' is a non sequitur; people do not achieve insight viscerally. When the client claims he or she has intellectual but not emotional insight, the therapist reinterprets this claim as either a problem of 'knowing' but not 'believing' the rational ideas, or of inconsistency of beliefs across time.
>
> (Walen et al. 1992: 216).

Knowing but not believing usually occurs because clients do not put their new knowledge into daily practice and therefore it is not integrated into their belief system. Inconsistency of beliefs across time means that in some situations a client might believe, for example, that it is not terrible to make mistakes, but it is terrible in other situations.

insults

Insults can hurt us if we agree with their intended aim to denigrate us or make us angry if we demand we should not be insulted. For example, a colleague says to you that you are 'a lazy bastard'. One way to handle insults is to ask yourself: are they justified? If it is true, then acknowledge you are not pulling your weight in the office ('Thank you for pointing it out to me, though the bastard bit was unnecessary') and state what steps you will take to correct it. If the accusation is untrue, then allow the other person the right to be wrong – believing you are 'a lazy bastard' is his problem, not yours. Alternatively, you can see the other person's false accusations as merely a difference of opinion (Hauck 1980b). In these ways, insults are 'defanged' and rendered harmless.

intuition

We see intuition as accumulated implicit knowledge rather than as knowledge acquired immediately without benefit of experience or reason. If you say that you like to 'work intuitively' or you 'intuitively understand what's going on with the client', you simply mean that you have a series of hunches derived from this implicit knowledge (we do not agree that intuition is 'a true and certain source of knowledge'). A hunch is a hypothesis and therefore needs to be confirmed, modified or disconfirmed in the light of what the data show, not on the basis of what your instinct might suggest. When you execute clinical interventions based on 'it just felt instinctively the right thing to do', we would reinterpret this instinct as rapid (or very rapid) information processing. This rapid information processing can be made explicit and 'slowed down' for discussion in supervision of your session audiotapes.

When clients claim intuitive truths about themselves (e.g. 'I just know that when people first meet me, they immediately dislike me'), would you automatically agree that this is reliable knowledge or wonder if there are cognitive distortions at work in the client's thinking which might emanate from underlying negative beliefs? When you or your client trust intuition as a source of 'true' knowledge, gather facts and information about the issue at hand and then reconsider if instinct is always reliable or true. This practice may demonstrate that good judgements or decisions sometimes turn out to be counter-intuitive.

irrationality

Irrationality is usually viewed as a rejection of reason. Whatever the complex scientific or philosophical views of what constitutes irrationality, our view of it is simple and straightforward: does a person's beliefs and actions help or hinder her in the attainment of her desired goals? For example, a person believes 'I'm not interesting enough' and avoids social opportunities in order not to be exposed as 'boring', whereas her goal is to have a more exciting life and develop self-confidence. The person is being irrational or self-defeating because her beliefs and behaviour militate against goal-attainment. Additionally, would she encourage her partner and/or children to adopt her beliefs and behaviour? The usual answer is 'No', because the person can see how counterproductive they are (e.g. 'I don't want my kids to become as screwed up as I am').

Help your clients to elicit the poor results from their irrational outlook (e.g. continuing social isolation) and re-evaluate its putative benefits (e.g. 'I suppose it keeps me safe from being rejected or ridiculed, but it also keeps me trapped in a joyless existence'). Through this process, clients develop self-helping and goal-directed beliefs and behaviours that underpin RATIONALITY.

'it does my head in'

A common expression and one that views external stressors as the cause of one's problems, e.g. 'I've got such a tight deadline to meet, it's doing my head in.' From the CBT perspective, what precisely is the 'it' referring to? Clarifying the 'it' enables you to understand the client's emotional and behavioural reactions to the stressor:

A = activating event – uncertainty about meeting a tight deadline
B = beliefs – 'If I miss the deadline, I'll be seen as incompetent. I couldn't bear to be seen like that.'
C = consequences – increasing anxiety and frenetic activity

What is 'doing her head in' is not A, the external stressor, but B, her evaluation of this stressor. It is B that largely produces the unpleasant consequences at C (see A–C THINKING, EMOTIONAL RESPONSIBILITY and EVALUATION). With B representing the 'it', the client can now see how 'I do my own head in'.

While it is undoubtedly important for her to meet the deadline, if she does miss it, she can learn to bear this setback without disturbance by separating performance evaluation from self-evaluation (e.g. 'I performed badly on this occasion, but my performance does not make me incompetent'). If some of her colleagues do see her as incompetent, they are making the same evaluation error as she was. In conclusion, if the 'it' is not clarified, therapy is likely to stray into less clinically relevant areas.

it–me confusion (Gilbert 2000)

This confusion occurs when we rate ourselves (ME) on the basis of our behaviour or performance (IT), e.g. 'I didn't get the job therefore I'm a failure.' As such, self-acceptance is conditional: 'I only accept ME if I do IT well' (Gilbert 2000: 107). This confusion is cleared up when we learn to see the self as unrateable, but not aspects of it, e.g. 'I was incompetent at doing IT, but this does not define ME' (see SELF-ACCEPTANCE).

'it's not my responsibility'

Some clients might say that the person(s) who 'caused' their problems should shoulder the responsibility for their recovery. For example, a client who takes time off work with depression due to constant bullying from several colleagues, asserts: 'My managers let it happen, so it's up to them to get me better. It's not my fault what happened to me.' However, the company does not accept responsibility/liability for his depression but the client insists that 'my recovery is in their hands'. Point out to such clients that no matter how their problems were caused, they need to take responsibility for tackling them. An analogy can reinforce this point:

> If your car burst into flames after being hit by another car, would you expect the other driver to rescue you from the flames or would you make a determined effort to save yourself? If you experienced panic attacks after being burgled, would you say that the burglar should now become your therapist or would you seek professional help if your own efforts proved unsuccessful?

This analogy is not meant to be facetious, but underscores the inescapable point that change starts to occur when personal responsibility is accepted for it.

'I've tried everything'

When clients say this, they usually mean they have exhausted their repertoire of skills in trying to overcome their problems. Your reply to this can be: 'You've tried everything that you know, but you haven't tried everything that I know. This means I can show you other ways of tackling your problems that might provide the breakthrough.' This declaration is not meant to be condescending or arrogant, but states a simple fact: you have considerable training and experience in dealing with emotional disorders which the client does not have; therefore, you have more to offer the client than he has to offer to himself. There might be occasions when you suggest things the client has already tried, but this time you add another element that the client overlooked – he did not persevere with his efforts at change (see PERSISTENCE).

jealousy

Bishay et al. distinguish morbid from normal jealousy: 'Morbid jealousy is used to signify an excessive irrational preoccupation with the partner's fidelity for which there is no objective foundation. Normal jealousy can therefore be defined as a jealousy reaction occurring when the partner is unfaithful' (1996: 9). In morbid jealousy, Hauck (1982a) suggests the real problem is not so much the person's distrust of his partner, but distrust of himself, i.e. he sees himself as inferior to potential or imagined rivals (e.g. 'I'm not good enough for you. How could you love or want me?') and believes the relationship is threatened when she talks to other men. Also, the person is intolerant of uncertainty regarding his partner's faithfulness (e.g. 'Is she having an affair with him? I've got to know!').

Show this client that if he wants to enjoy the relationship he is continually afraid of losing, then he needs to stop making his self-worth conditional on being loved (e.g. 'Without love, I'm worthless') and accept the fact that there will always be other men who are better looking, more charming, richer than he is, but that does not mean his partner will go off with them. His intolerance of uncertainty needs to be countered with evidence-based estimates of the likelihood of her infidelity (e.g. 'We've been together for ten years, we have four children and things seem reasonably stable. So far, so good').

If the relationship does end, that is not the end of him because he no longer believes the old song 'You're nobody until somebody loves you', but prefers to sing 'You're still somebody even if nobody loves you'. This new outlook is much less likely to stir morbid jealousy when he eventually finds a new relationship.

Jesus Christ (as judge)

If a Christian client says she cannot forgive herself for past wrongdoings (e.g. lying to her best friend, being unfaithful to her husband), then point out that Jesus Christ forgives her. He may condemn the sin but not the sinner, so why is she putting herself above His teachings? Is she vain enough to believe her judgement is superior to His? The human condition is one of fallibility and any number of transgressions are capable of God's forgiveness; in fact, 'there can never be so great a number [of wrongdoings] that it cuts us off from the forgiveness or love of God' (Mathews 2000: 13). By accepting her fallibility because Christ does, she can start moderating the intense guilt she still feels about past events.

judge and jury

Encourage your clients to act as a judge or jury member in a court case in examining their negative beliefs: 'Try to decide whether a belief is true or false by considering the belief in isolation from what it makes you feel. Is the belief true or false according to the facts? You should not decide whether a belief is true or false based on how it makes you feel' (Free 1999: 86). For example, a client says she feels 'tormented by guilt' because she left her alcoholic husband who then drank himself to death – 'I killed him by deserting him when he really needed me.'

A crucial issue for the client to consider is this: if she could not stop her husband drinking when she was living with him (and she tried many times), how did she acquire the power to kill him when she left him? She can only attempt to influence him, nothing greater than that. An objective analysis of the situation (i.e. separating feelings from facts) can then be delivered by the client-as-judge in summing up her own case: 'My husband was an alcoholic. I did my best to help but to no avail. Eventually, I found our life together intolerable, so I left him. My departure helped to hasten his death but certainly did not cause it. His death still saddens me, but I no longer feel guilty about it.'

jumping to conclusions

Suggest to your clients that they walk towards a conclusion rather than jump to it, i.e. carefully evaluate evidence in order to reach a balanced judgement instead of a hasty one. For example, after the first session a client says, 'Therapy isn't working'. As well as finding out why the client has reached this conclusion so early on in therapy, suggest to him that a more suitable timescale for evaluation might be after six sessions of collaborative work including the carrying out of homework assignments.

just reasonable contentment (Hauck 1983)

Some clients might be uncertain whether or not to stay in a relationship. A starting point for discussion can be the concept of just reasonable contentment (JRC):

> The goal of a relationship is to see to it that you remain at least just reasonably content at all times and that you have hope for a greater degree of contentment. When the parties involved can all say that they are reasonably content there is obviously little reason to complain, and each party is bound to be pleased with the other party.
>
> (Hauck 1983: 37)

When an individual falls below the JRC level, dissatisfaction outweighs contentment, she can tackle her dissatisfaction constructively in an attempt to return to the JRC level or, if this is unsuccessful, consider leaving the relationship and removing any blocks (e.g. guilt) that prevent her from doing so.

just world-view

An individual's assumptions about the world (e.g. 'Bad things don't happen to good people') can be shattered by traumatic events (Janoff-Bulman 1992). A typical response to such events is the question, 'Why me?' Implicit in this question is the belief that the world should be fair and just (Lerner 1980; see FALLACY). Helping your clients to make sense of their traumatic experience is an important step in their recovery. Wanting a just world is a laudable ideal, but unfairness is part of life and there is no way at present to avoid or remove it. Integrating the trauma into a new or modified outlook can help clients to accept their misfortune and still find some happiness and meaning in life (e.g. 'Kindness to others is no guarantee of protection from nasty things in life. I might be mugged again but this possibility is not going to make me cynical or less charitable towards others'). Thus,

> . . . the question 'Why me?' may be answered by the therapist with 'Why not me?' not in a flip or minimizing way, but to begin discussion concerning the fact that unfortunate [or tragic] events can occur to anyone.
>
> (Warren and Zgourides 1991: 154-55)

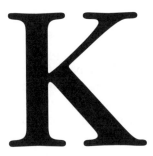

'kangaroo' thinking

This refers to clients who jump from problem to problem (hopping about all over the place). Needless to say, little productive work can be accomplished if they refuse to settle on one problem (e.g. 'Everything needs looking at. How can I focus on work problems when my relationship is falling apart, I've got colossal debts and my brother-in-law is suing me?'). Suggest to such clients that 'digestive' thinking (i.e. chewing the cud) can replace 'kangaroo' thinking' as this is more likely to start the process of constructive problem-solving. Problems and possible solutions to them are now examined in a systematic and focused way. This helps to stop the previously unrestricted roaming of clients' attention.

'King Canute' thinking

King Canute tried to make the incoming tide go back in order to prove to his obsequious courtiers that kings have limited powers because they are only human. The popular myth about the king is that he thought he could turn back the tide. This entry focuses on the myth. Just because a person thinks he has immense power or authority, the world will not automatically obey him. In fact, the world will not obey anyone, powerful or not. We engage in 'King Canute' thinking when we demand that the world bends to our will (e.g. 'I must have what I want in life'; 'My career path must not be blocked in any way'). No matter how strongly we demand that the world must be how we want it to be, it does not change to accommodate our demands and commands. Accepting our LIMITATIONS allows us to distinguish between what we can and cannot change about the world.

knowledge

Clients often insist that they know something to be true, e.g. 'Look, I know for a fact that you can't be happy without a partner. Now there it is.' What is the epistemological basis for this 'fact'? The client might say, for example, that his parents told him or 'Everyone knows that you become miserable living alone' (see AUTHORITARIAN EPISTEMOLOGY). The client's 'truth' may prove self-limiting in not helping him to cope constructively with the end of his relationship.

You can help him to widen his knowledge base, and thereby increase his options, by encouraging him to become a scientific collaborator in examining the validity of his current beliefs and developing alternative, self-helping beliefs. For example, the client now concedes that his parents defined happiness too narrowly and 'everyone' is actually some of his friends who also coped poorly when their relationships finished. Experimenting with living alone has taught him that 'it isn't too bad really, though I would prefer eventually to be in another relationship'. Obtaining knowledge in more reliable and valid ways by adopting a scientific epistemology enables clients to form new conceptualizations of themselves and the world.

labelling

Clients frequently attach depreciatory labels to themselves on the basis of their actions (e.g. 'I made a mistake, so I'm stupid'). Labelling is inaccurate because it cannot capture the complexity of the self and unhelpful as it is unlikely to motivate clients to change. Teaching clients to label their behaviours rather than themselves means they are less likely to give themselves a hard time when things go wrong (e.g. 'I made a mistake, too bad, but I'm not stupid because of it') and more likely to try to put things right.

Labelling can be used as a bolt-hole from problem-solving (e.g. 'If I'm no good, then what's the point of trying to achieve anything worthwhile in my life?'). Encouraging clients to face instead of retreat from their problems can start with explaining the cop-out clause: 'This involves letting yourself off the hook from trying to achieve anything worthwhile in life by calling yourself "no good". Now, what would you like to achieve for yourself if you gave up putting yourself down and started channelling your energies in a positive direction?'

learning

As part of their developing role as a self-therapist or coach, encourage your clients to take responsibility for their own learning (assisted by you, of course). Instead of learning in a haphazard way, introduce your clients to the learning cycle (Kolb 1984; Honey and Mumford 1992), 'which explains all the stages you need to undertake in order to have a complete learning experience' (Jones 1998: 77).

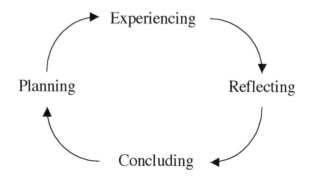

For example, a client feels anxious about speaking up at meetings or in groups because she fears being exposed as 'stupid for saying the wrong things':

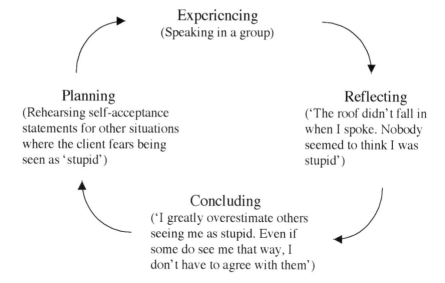

Suggest to your clients that they keep a learning diary, so that going through the learning cycle becomes an automatic response to new situations and experiences. In this way, clients' learning is owned by them rather than handed over by you (which some clients might have expected when they entered therapy).

The above model helps clients to learn how to learn. However, some clients may fail to profit from their experiences and keep repeating the same mistakes. As Beck et al. observe: 'This is a central problem in all forms of therapy because of the human tendency to repeat the same self-destructive patterns' (1985a: 187). Launching into therapy without removing these learning blocks, or not noticing them when they occur, means that the client's presenting problems will not be addressed successfully. For example, a client who believed she was inadequate kept taking on tasks beyond her level of competence which inevitably resulted in failure and emphatic reconfirmation of her self-image.

As Beck et al. state: 'A large part of the problem is that a person is unaware of having a closed mind' (1985a: 187). Learning and closed-mindedness are obviously incompatible for a successful therapeutic outcome. In the above example, for learning to learn to begin, the client stopped denigrating herself, strove to achieve SELF-ACCEPTANCE, focused on carrying out tasks within her current level of competence, and carefully evaluated the outcome (e.g. 'I suppose, after all, I can do some things adequately if I pick the right tasks'). In this way, learning started to work its way into her previously closed mind.

lies (client)

If you believe your client is telling lies, it is inadvisable to confront him in a hostile fashion (e.g. 'Look, I know you're lying. You're still taking the drugs!'). Instead, Beck et al. suggest that you 'develop a repertoire of carefully worded statements that "nicely" say the equivalent of "I think your lying" . . . [e.g.] 'I don't get the feeling you're being completely straight with me right now' (1993: 78). You can also bring up the issue of lying directly:

> Let's assume for the moment that you are lying. What will be the likely consequences for you if therapy is based on lies rather than on honesty? Admitting to lying doesn't have to mean therapy is terminated but we don't want to waste time either. So, how shall we proceed then?

If a client believes he is 'getting away with it' or 'pulling the wool over your eyes', explain to him that he is not 'getting away with it' because all he is doing is postponing addressing his problems and they may actually get worse during this postponement period. As for being deceived, this will not stop you from enjoying your life – is he enjoying his?

limitations

Saying we all have our limitations seems straightforward enough. However, admitting to them without self-condemnation may be another matter. For example, a person who finds that he can no longer complete a marathon states that he is 'now only fit for the knacker's yard'. He neglects to consider important factors for his lack of stamina such as previous injuries, declining health and advancing age. On the other hand, another person might be too ready to concede his limitations, e.g. 'I started that course but I gave it up because I realized I haven't got the brain power for it.' In this case, the person may have stopped the course through lack of effort, not intellectual ability.

Assessing our capabilities needs to be done objectively: what is beyond our competence, what is and what could be within it. Our energies can then be channelled into the last two categories (in the first example, the person grudgingly accepted that he would delay the 'knacker's yard' solution as he could still run half-marathons; in the second example, the person gave the course 'another go').

logic

Priest suggests that 'most people like to think of themselves as logical' (2000: 1). Clients who consider themselves to be logically-minded often produce highly illogical statements, e.g. 'My boss criticized my performance, so that means I'm incompetent' (see PART–WHOLE ERROR). Does the conclusion ('I'm incompetent') follow logically from the premiss ('My boss criticized my performance')? In other words, is the conclusion true? Helping your clients to understand how they arrived at their illogical conclusions highlights their process of reasoning and what corrections need to be made to it. Explain to them that applying greater intellectual rigour to their reasoning will result in fewer *non sequiturs*, which, in turn, will reduce the occurrence of self-disturbance. We hope your clients will see that as sound reasoning.

loneliness

Living alone and having no close friends do not automatically lead to experiencing disturbed feelings like depression and anger (though clients often claim that they do). What does lead to disturbed feelings are the personal meanings clients attach to these circumstances (e.g. 'Why can't I be living with someone or going out every night with friends? I must be inadequate and unlovable to be living in a way that I don't want to'). Loneliness can be seen as living alone with self-depreciation as a constant factor in this existence. Though it is easier said than done, solitude does not have to be an oppressive experience, but one that clients can learn to embrace. As Butler and Hope observe:

> To be at ease with yourself, alone, can be a source of refreshment and energy . . . Solitude is not the opposite of good relationships. Indeed, if we

are continually seeking company because we are uncomfortable with ourselves, this is likely to tarnish our relationships. If we are at ease with ourselves, we will be at ease with others.

(Butler and Hope 1996: 124)

Loneliness can be banished if clients stop denigrating themselves for living alone and see their own company as something to enjoy instead of endure. Developing vitally absorbing interests can help them to make profitable use of their 'home alone' time. Increased self-confidence allows clients to forge closer relationships and find a suitable partner based on genuine interest and desire, not to keep loneliness at bay.

As well as self-depreciation, loneliness can also involve LOW FRUSTRA-TION TOLERANCE (e.g. 'It's intolerable living alone'). Coping with living alone can be made bearable through learning HIGH FRUSTRATION TOLERANCE (e.g. 'I don't like being on my own but I can tolerate it'). If some clients say that loneliness is like solitary confinement, then an LFT attitude is likely to break them psychologically while an HFT outlook will help them to adapt to and survive the experience until brighter times emerge.

loss

Experiencing some form of loss (e.g. hope, self-esteem, partner) is probably unavoidable. However, this loss can be compounded by refusing to accept that it has occurred. For example, a person whose business had collapsed became depressed: 'I worked so incredibly hard to build it up. I cannot accept that it's gone. Without the business, I'm a failure. What's the point in trying again or even going on?' In this example, the person has suffered a double loss – of his business and of his ability to adapt psychologically to it.

On the other hand, a loss can be coupled with a benefit (though the person might take some time to see it in this way). The benefit is psychological adaptation to the loss, which, in turn, is more likely to engender sadness than depression. This adaptation means the person does not feel hopeless about the future, recognizes that experiencing loss is part of the complex business of living and integrates this knowl-edge into a wider view of the world (Dryden 1994b). Sadness helps the person to grieve, move on and encourages him to take constructive action (e.g. becoming an employee again). Depression or psycholog-ical maladaptation tends either to inhibit or extend the grieving process and militates against taking constructive action (e.g. the person sits at home waiting for his business to be miraculously revived).

low frustration tolerance

Low frustration tolerance (LFT) is based on a person's perceived inability to tolerate or withstand unpleasant events or frustrating circumstances, e.g. 'I can't stand boring meetings'; 'I can't bear being lied to'; 'It's intolerable that he can be so rude to me'. Such statements suggest the person is going to disintegrate: how can she keep mind and body intact in the face of these 'terrible' situations? Such statements are grossly exaggerated because the person has 'stood it', albeit not very well, time and time again. Another way of proving to clients that they can stand what they believe they cannot, is to ask them under what conditions this could occur (possible reply: 'If you gave me a million pounds!'). Learning to tolerate adverse events without emotional and behavioural disturbance leads to HIGH FRUSTRATION TOLERANCE.

luck

Some clients might complain that they have no luck in life, e.g. 'My friend always lands on her feet. I never do. I suppose I'm just not lucky.' On closer inspection, her friend's luck may owe more to calculation than chance if it means labouring under controlled knowledge (LUCK). This kind of luck is based on hard work, self-discipline and learning from mistakes; therefore, the person can to some degree control what happens to her – hence the expression, 'You make your own luck'. The 'unlucky' person often lacks these aforementioned qualities and may drift through life hoping for a 'lucky break' to give meaning to his life (e.g. winning the National Lottery). Transforming luck into LUCK starts with setting personally significant goals and being committed to the hard work and learning necessary to reach them.

magical thinking

The idea that desirable effects or results can be achieved simply by wishing them to exist (Dryden and Neenan 1995). For example, a client might believe: 'I shouldn't have to work hard to get what I want. It should be there for the taking.' Such thinking is like sucking on a dummy: it provides comfort but does not promote change. Getting rid of the dummy means exchanging magical thinking for a realistic outlook: namely, that change is often effortful rather than effortless.

magnification

When clients magnify their problems, a sense of proportion is lost. For example, a person is mildly criticized by his partner; he concludes that she has destroyed his character. Imagery can help clients to remember to keep events within a realistic perspective: 'When a dog barks at you is it transformed into the Hound of the Baskervilles or do a few spots of rain become a torrential downpour?' (see MINIMIZATION).

maintenance of gains from therapy

Once your clients have achieved their GOALS, this is not the end of the therapeutic story although many of them will think or hope that it is (Dryden and Yankura 1995). If clients want to maintain their gains after therapy has ended, they need to continue to implement the principles and techniques they learnt in therapy. Progress will not continue unaided and, therefore, lapses or relapses are more likely to occur if clients 'take their eye off the ball'. Emphasize that 'continuing improvement means continuing input' from them.

manipulation

When clients complain of being manipulated by others, the issue to focus on is why they allow themselves to be manipulated (see EMOTIONAL BLACK-MAIL). For example, a client says that her partner manipulates her into supporting his decisions by 'playing on my lack of education and his university degree'. The client reveals that lack of education means she is inferior and she feels self-conscious in the presence of someone educated – 'I feel I don't have a right to my opinions because I'm thick'. The client equates intelligence with academic achievement rather than seeing it as consisting of a number of different abilities (e.g. she does the DIY jobs around the house as her partner lacks the patience and skill to help her or do them himself).

By re-evaluating the concept of intelligence, she no longer sees herself as 'thick' and inferior: 'If I think you're right, I'll go along with the decision; if I think you're wrong, I'll say so. I'm not articulate like you, but I know in my own mind what's right and wrong.' Help your clients to isolate and tackle the ideas that make them vulnerable to manipulation.

meaning

Eliciting the meaning a client attaches to events in her life helps you to understand her emotional reaction to these events. Meaning provides you with entry into the client's internal world and enhances empathy. Some clients might be curious to know why you seem to be so interested in the 'meaning of things'. You could reply: 'If I don't understand what things mean to you, then I'll be conducting meaningless therapy, so to speak. Also, by pursuing meaning you might become aware of more information which will help us to build a more complete picture of your problems.' Without meaning, you are on the outside trying to look in and the client is on the inside looking out and wondering if you really understand what is going on with her.

means–ends thinking

This refers to 'articulating the sequences of step-by-step means that may be necessary to carry out a particular solution to a . . . problem' (Platt et al. 1986: 267). In other words, planning how to get from here (current state) to there (goal state) and removing obstacles along the way. Means–ends thinking can be likened to a journey: you want to get from London to Glasgow (Glasgow is your end); so you consider the different ways of getting there (means) and evaluate the advantages and disadvantages of each method before choosing the most appropriate.

mental filter

When clients process information through a mental filter, they dwell on a negative detail instead of seeing the bigger picture; this detail eventually contaminates their view of the bigger picture. In order to replace tunnel vision with a panoramic view of events, ask your clients to step back mentally and carefully appraise the whole situation. For example, you might say: 'I know you're focused on yesterday's plane crash and therefore you believe that air travel is incredibly dangerous; however, if you compare plane crashes per year with number of flights per year, you can come to a very different conclusion – that airlines have a good safety record rather than a horrendous one.' In this way, information processing becomes fair-minded instead of fixated.

mental laziness

This involves not thinking for yourself or letting others spoon-feed you with their ideas (see GULLIBILITY, 'GURU' THINKING, 'I DON'T KNOW' and SUGGESTIBILITY). Mental laziness leads to mental stagnation; so trying to form your own opinions can seem like a Herculean task. A shrug of the shoulders or an 'I don't know' becomes a safe and effortless way to keep others at bay when they ask, for example, 'Surely you've got something to say about it'. Do not collude with mentally lazy clients by supplying them with the answers to your questions.

No doubt some clients will become irritated when you urge them to 'think things through for yourself' or persist with 'I'd like to hear your opinion on this subject'. At least irritability indicates that something is stirring in the stagnation: 'Therapy is useless!' You can ask the client to expand on his statement with examples of the 'uselessness of therapy', followed by a discussion on how therapy can be constructively improved to help him (remaining taciturn is not viewed by you as a constructive improvement). Combating mental laziness means letting the client's brain take more of the strain in therapy.

meta-emotional problems (Dryden 1995)

These are secondary emotional problems that clients develop in relation to their primary emotional problems (e.g. ashamed of feeling anxious; guilty about displaying anger). When meta-emotions are involved, clients are giving themselves two problems for the price of one: instead of attempting to lighten their emotional load, they end up making it heavier. Meta-emotional problems distract clients from working on their primary problems, hold back their progress and extend their time in therapy. Meta-emotional problems can be removed quickly if clients stop condemning themselves for their primary problems, as in the above examples, 'I'm weak' (shame) and 'I'm bad' (guilt). Self-condemnation adds nothing of value to problem-solving.

mindfulness

This means mentally stepping back and observing one's own thinking. Are there ideas that you cling to that have outlived their usefulness or need to be modified? If you keep on making the same or similar errors, what prevents you LEARNING from these errors? What things in life bring you happiness? Mindfulness is minding one's own mental business, taking time out to examine one's mental life. Mindfulness counters 'mindlessness' (i.e. avoiding reflective thinking) and provides 'quiet time' for individuals who claim 'I'm always so busy. I haven't got time to think!'

mind-reading

Mind-reading can be seen as a form of projection: 'The thoughts patients believe others are having about them are usually the very thoughts they are having about themselves' (Persons 1989: 113). For example, if a client thinks he is boring, then he is likely to conclude that others will see him in the same way. Emphasize to your client that it is important for him to read his own mind instead of other people's, and read his own mind in a non-distorted way: 'What evidence do I have that I am boring? How did I form this opinion of myself? If some people actually tell me that I am boring, does that make them right about me?'

minimization

Minimization is akin to giving yourself a reference for a job in which you highlight your weaknesses and downplay your strengths. A prospective employer might wonder if she is having her leg pulled. If you wrote a similar reference for a friend, he might consider suing you! Minimization means, 'I've got nothing good to say about myself.' To which you can reply: 'You have, but you're not trying hard enough' (see MAGNIFICATION).

misattribution

This involves attributing one's problem to the wrong cause, e.g. 'I don't have any friends because I don't like going to pubs'. Friends can be found in other locations, not just pubs, and if all the pubs were closed down, would the person then be able to make friends? The person's lack of friends can be attributed to the right cause: his shyness and fear of rejection. In order to help your clients attribute their problems to more likely causes, collaboratively compile a list of possible causes and separate the plausible from the implausible.

models

When a client says 'I wish I could be like her [best friend]. She carries herself with such poise and confidence', she is setting herself an impossible goal – the client cannot make herself an exact copy of her best friend. What she can do by observing her best friend's behaviour is to extract from it information that she can then use to improve her own poise and confidence. If she keeps on engaging in wistful thinking, she will stay yearning, but not learning.

motivation

Motivation may be much discussed by you and the client, but little analysed. Also, clients may have their own idiosyncratic definition of the term (e.g. 'Wanting to change, if it isn't too difficult'; 'I turn up and you sort me out'). Explaining how psychologists understand the concept of motivation can help clients to see the possible shortcomings in their own version of it. Motivation is made up of three components (Arnold et al. 1998: 245):

1. direction – what a person is trying to do.
2. effort – how hard a person is trying.
3. persistence – how long a person continues trying.

A client may have a direction, applies effort, but lacks PERSISTENCE (a frequent reason why clients drop out of therapy). Client are more likely to achieve their goals when all three components are in evidence. Motivation can be summarized as 'trying hard and long'.

It seems logical to assume that a person cannot be expected to carry out a task if he is not motivated to do it (e.g. filling in his tax return), and this assumption applies with even greater force if the person is depressed. However, as Emery observes in discussing depression:

> . . . motivation works backwards. At first you're unmotivated; but, if you take action anyway, you *then* begin to feel motivated. Paradoxically, you only feel like taking action after you have already taken some. Make the aim not to do

something, or to have something, but simply to take action and see what happens.

(Emery 2000: 37; original author's emphasis)

For clients who subscribe to the 'I can't do it until I'm motivated' hypothesis, ask them to put it to the test – take action in the absence of motivation. The results are likely to prove to them that they have been putting the cart before the horse, i.e. action comes before motivation, not after it (Burns 1989; see also CART-BEFORE-THE-HORSE THINKING).

musts

Rigid musts (e.g. 'I must have your love'; 'I must not display any weaknesses') are a form of dictatorial thinking – no dissent is allowed. The person lets herself become subservient to the centralized control of the musts. Musts might make sense if they were frequently met – yet they infrequently are. Even when a must is achieved, like gaining love as in the above example, the person remains vulnerable as she is anxious about losing it. If love is lost, the person usually pays the price of the must through emotional disturbance, e.g. she becomes depressed because she concludes that she is worthless without love or cannot envisage tolerating a loveless existence.

The client can start a cognitive revolt by asking herself, 'Why must I?', and looking for evidence to confirm or disconfirm her musts, e.g. 'Musts are self-created fictions, not established facts'. Through such detailed examination, the client can install a benign and flexible system of thinking which allows her to pursue her goals but not to her detriment if they are unrealizable or transient, e.g. 'I very much want to be loved, but there is no reason why I must be loved. I can still be reasonably happy and prosper in life if love proves elusive or fleeting.' Absolute SHOULDS (e.g. 'I absolutely should not have shouted at my son and I'm a terrible mother for doing so') also require eviction from our thinking for the same reasons as the musts.

needs

Some needs are indisputable: without food, water, shelter, air, we will die. These needs apply to everyone equally and transcend any beliefs we have about how to conduct our lives or what goals to seek. Beyond these objective needs, other needs can be seen as subjective (i.e. self-created). When a person says he needs love, approval, sex, an interesting job or the respect of his peers, he really means he desires these things, and no matter how powerful his desires are, they do not become transformed into objective needs. If his subjective needs are not met, he will not suffer the same fate as when his objective needs are not satisfied.

Subjective needs can be limitless (e.g. 'I must have *those* trainers. The cheaper ones will make me look like a peasant. I couldn't bear that'). By describing desires as needs the person creates the impression that there is something wrong with his life or himself and this can only be remedied through the fulfilment of that need (e.g. 'I can't be happy living in this flat. I need to move now. When's the council going to get its bloody finger out?'). Believing you need something leads to acting as if you do, sometimes with tragic consequences, e.g. a person kills herself because 'I can't live without love'. In this example, her death has become a self-fulfilling prophecy: she equated love with water or food – vital for her survival and happiness.

Helping clients to distinguish between needs and desires starts with their language, e.g. 'When you say "I need her approval", what you really mean is "I desire her approval, but I don't need it".' You can then explore with them the likely emotional reactions to not getting what they believe they need versus not getting what they desire. Clients are usually able to imagine the more intense emotional reactions they would experience when their needs are not met.

Self-created needs can never be satisfied because the person believes he can never get enough of what he believes he needs (Emery 2000), e.g. 'Who can be happy without money? I never miss an opportunity to make money' (when he does miss opportunities, he thinks he is in dire financial straits and views his life as miserable). Needs can feel like compulsions (e.g. 'I have to lose weight. There is no other choice'). Changing needs into wants banishes compulsion and replaces it with choice (e.g. 'I want to lose weight, but I can see that it's not a necessity to do so'). From the REBT perspective, needs can be seen as a subclass of MUSTS.

neurotic agreement in therapy (Hauck 1966)

This means that you agree with your client's maladaptive ideas (e.g. 'She's right: you are worthless without a partner'). Indications that you are subscribing to the neurotic agreement include (Dryden 1994a):

- Feeling uncomfortable when the client discusses these 'shared' ideas and seeking ways to shift her attention elsewhere.
- Being tentative when challenging your client's maladaptive beliefs (the tentativeness is not due to skills deficits in challenging these beliefs).
- You attack the client's belief instead of non-confrontationally challenging it. This may occur as a form of projection or you may actually hate yourself for holding such ideas and thereby hate the client for reminding you of your own inadequacies.

Opting out of the neurotic agreement starts with becoming aware of your self-defeating ideas (e.g. by examining your own uncomfortable feelings when the client mentions certain subjects, listening to audio-tapes of sessions, discussing your difficulties with your supervisor), accepting yourself for holding these ideas and forming adaptive ideas instead (e.g. 'I'm a person in my own right with or without a partner, though it's preferable to have a partner'). A new agreement you conclude with yourself is to keep your clinical attention focused on the client (the neurotic agreement means you were putting your own concerns first). Your own material is to be dealt with outside of therapy (Neenan and Dryden 1996).

'no'

When clients start standing up for themselves in their domestic, social and/or work-based relationships, it is important that they do not use saying 'No' as a form of revenge to compensate for their past excessive compliance (e.g. 'I hated myself for being so spineless. It's payback time now!'). Saying 'No', politely but firmly, is part of the client's new rational outlook: he no longer NEEDS the approval, friendship or respect of others, or fears or avoids interpersonal strife; if others upset themselves when he says 'No' to them, that is their problem, not his; and his interests are just as important as anyone else's. When the client now says 'Yes' to a request, there is no sense of compulsion on his part and when he says 'No', he does not feel guilty.

'no one cares about me'

To this despairing observation, you can ask: 'Does that include you?' If it is true that no one cares about the client, then this has to include the client himself. Maybe attempts to elicit caring behaviour from others have been rebuffed, so the client's last resort is to learn to develop self-care, i.e. treat himself as he would somebody he cared about. As Davidson remarks, some clients 'have little idea about how to go about caring for themselves' (2000: 100). Planning a programme of self-care can involve doing more of what the client already enjoys (e.g. reading, listening to music), developing an exercise programme, getting an animal for a companion and organizing a daily activity schedule.

You can discuss with the client how lacking a philosophy of self-care is signalling to others that 'I don't think much of myself'. This can lead to others treating him with disdain (e.g. 'Why should I care about you when you don't care about yourself? You're not my responsibility'), exploiting him in some way or being scared away by his 'neediness' thereby exhausting any residual sympathy they feel for him. The eventual result is often social isolation. When the client starts to care for himself, and this will be evident in his manner, dress, bearing, outlook, he can no longer claim 'No one cares for me'. Then it is likely that others will start to take an interest in him.

'no win' situation

This occurs when clients believe change will be just as unsatisfactory as staying the way they are (e.g. 'My relationship is boring, but if I leave I'll probably end up lonely. Can't win, can I?'). The client 'can't win' with the way he has constructed his choices: enduring boredom or embracing LONELINESS. 'No win' thinking is often disturbance-inducing (e.g. 'Depressed if I stay and depressed if I leave').

Developing a rounded view of life instead of clinging to a simple one would allow the client to see a range of choices before him. For example, he could try to reinvigorate his relationship rather than stay slumped in boredom or he could experiment with living alone in order to realize that it does not have to result in loneliness. As long as the client is prepared to expend effort, take risks and accept uncertainty (about what lies ahead), he is more likely to start 'winning', i.e. getting more enjoyment out of his life (see DILEMMA).

non-compliance

When clients do not carry out their homework tasks, elicit from them the reasons for their non-compliance and what steps are required for compliance to occur. However, when clients consistently refuse to carry out homework, emphasize what the bottom line of non-compliance is: compliance to maintain the status quo (i.e. stay emotionally disturbed). You can distinguish between thinking non-compliance and non-thinking non-compliance:

> Thinking non-compliance means you have carefully considered the consequences for yourself if you don't do the homework and you are prepared to accept these consequences. Non-thinking non-compliance means you are simply not going to do the homework tasks but you haven't considered the consequences for yourself of not doing them.

If the client says at the next session, 'I was thinking about what you said last week . . .', you can mark this down as her first completed homework task even if she chooses not to stay in therapy.

'not yet'

This might be the client's reply to your suggestion that she start tackling her problems today. She might add, 'I'm not in the mood. The time doesn't feel right. I'll do it tomorrow or the day after when I'm feeling better.' The client's reluctance to start problem-solving today can be seen as an hypothesis she is trying to prove ('When I feel better tomorrow, then I'll get on with it'). You can suggest that she should try to disconfirm the hypothesis, not try to confirm it, by engaging in some tasks now. If she continues to procrastinate, confirmatory hypothesis-testing will always be a day away.

'nothing happened'

This is a common reply when clients are asked about their attempts to think and act differently. Usually 'something has happened' but the client is seeking rapid, easy or spectacular change and overlooks or dismisses what change has occurred. For example, a client with social anxiety agreed to go a party instead of avoiding it; she feared that her nervousness would reveal her as 'inadequate'. In reviewing the homework task, the client said: 'I didn't feel relaxed at all. I felt awkward and self-conscious all evening. I didn't have a good time and I couldn't wait to get home. It turned out just as I predicted.'

The client may have thought and behaved as before *at* the party, but the change was in choosing to go to it. Even though the outcome was disastrous from the client's viewpoint, this does not erase the choice she made. Why she failed to apply at the party the anxiety-reduction techniques learnt in the session remains to be investigated (e.g. the client may have behaved in the way she predicted she would).

'nothing works'

When clients say this about all the problem-solving techniques they have tried, do not gloomily or quickly concede that they are right. It is true that treatment in CBT is based on the experimental method and 'a variety of techniques may be tested until an effective one is found' (Beck et al. 1985: 189). These authors caution therapists not to abandon techniques without a sufficient trial – this caution applies equally to clients. If the client does abandon a technique too quickly, you can ask the following questions: did she understand the rationale for the technique? How much effort did she expend in executing the technique and how long did she persist with its execution? What LEARNING did she derive from trying the technique and was this learning used to inform her next attempt?

In this example, the client says that being assertive 'did not work because when I gave my opinion at the meeting, no one agreed with me' (the rationale for assertion is to speak up for oneself, not for others to agree with one's opinions). Expenditure of effort was minimal ('I sort of slipped my opinion in quickly and quietly') and persistence was absent ('I didn't say anything else'). The learning the client derived from the experience was 'to keep quiet in order to avoid being humiliated again'. In discussing these issues with the client, she conceded that she was expecting 'too much, too soon and I misunderstood what assertion really means'. She agreed to persevere with her assertion training. If nothing truly works, then the client cannot be helped; something usually works if the client is sufficiently open-minded and committed to finding out what it is.

Ockham's razor

This means that if something can be explained 'adequately without introducing further complexity, then the simple explanation is the best explanation' (Warburton 2000: 97). In CBT terms, if a client's problems can be resolved by correcting distortions in her thinking, then do not complicate matters by assuming you have got to tackle the probable source of the distortions – core beliefs. Only consider moving to deeper levels of cognition if warranted by the circumstances of the particular case.

Whether the complexity is introduced by you or the client, use the razor to cut through, among other things, verbiage, jargon, lengthy abstract discussions, complicated theories of emotional or behavioural causation (see CUTTING TO THE CHASE). For example, fear of spiders can be overcome quickly in a few sessions of graded exposure. The razor would need to be applied if the client wanted to explore endlessly how her fear of spiders originated or what the real meaning of her fear is (e.g. 'Is it really spiders I'm afraid of or is it some deeper, darker fear that I'm unwilling to face up to?'). To which you might reply: 'Let's deal with the spiders first. We'll see what happens after that.' Keeping things simple does not mean allowing simplism to creep into an explanation. As Naugle and Follette remark:

> While we favor simple explanations, it should be noted that the law of parsimony [another term for Ockham's razor] specifies the simplest *sufficient* explanation for a stated purpose. Thus, there is nothing inconsistent within a multifactor explanation for a set of clinical issues if they produce a better outcome than a simpler but less effective outcome.
>
> (1998: 67; original authors' emphasis)

For example, a client might attribute his current depression to losing his job a year ago. While losing his job may have triggered the start of his difficulties, what has been maintaining them over the past year would also need to be explored (e.g. the client might believe that without a job 'I'm not a real man'). Several or more factors are likely to be implicated in his depression rather than the single one he points to.

open-mindedness

How do we view ourselves, others and the world? Do we process incoming information in order to reinforce our existing beliefs and assumptions or do we allow ourselves to be receptive to considering or developing alternative viewpoints? Open-mindedness is editing out or reducing bias in our thinking such as 'I'm superior to everyone else' or 'You can never trust people with narrow eyes' (see PREJUDICE). Bias is maintained by cognitive distortions such as ALWAYS AND NEVER THINKING, MENTAL FILTER and MIND-READING.

Open-mindedness suggests that our judgements should be balanced ones (i.e. based on facts and sound reasoning), that our opinions can change when we examine *both* sides of an issue, and that we actively search for new ways of understanding and tackling our problems. (Baron et al. 1990 suggest that *too* much open-mindedness can lead to indecisiveness.) We readily acknowledge that human fallibility limits the degree of individual open-mindedness, but reducing our closed-mindedness as much as we can will allow for more 'safe landings' in our thinking, i.e. our thinking is less likely to lead to emotional disturbance. Providing 'safe landings' likens the mind to a parachute: it works best when it is open.

'ostrich' thinking

This occurs when a client buries his head in the sand and refuses to accept unpalatable facts in his life (e.g. his wife is planning to leave him). He will not be able to bury his head in the sand indefinitely as unfolding events will probably precipitate some sort of crisis for him (e.g. he threatens to kill himself as his wife is walking out the door). His 'ostrich-head' promotes self-delusion, but another part of the ostrich's anatomy, the stomach, will help him to face unpleasant reality because the ostrich is reputedly able to digest anything. (The connection here is with 'digestive' thinking; we are not claiming that you can think with your stomach!) If the client can digest unpalatable facts, then he can look at ways of coping constructively before and after his wife leaves (see DIGESTING).

overgeneralizing

A client who is turned down for a job believes 'I'll never be able to get a job'. The conclusion is unwarranted because it is based on inadequate data (one rejection). Overgeneralization underuses precision in the client's thinking. To counter this, ask the client to describe accurately his current circumstances and future prospects (e.g. 'I didn't get this job but I might get the next one'). Even if the client is turned down for ten jobs, this fact does not now justify his previous sweeping conclusion (e.g. 'I told you so'). The evidence might indicate the client is not qualified for the jobs he is applying for or has poor interview skills.

overlearning

This means that 'skills developed to the point where they are largely autonomous and rely very little on conscious processes for execution are much more resistant to deterioration' (Arnold et al. 1998: 373). Clients can overlearn through repetition why certain of their existing ideas (e.g. 'I'm a failure') are maladaptive and why new alternative ideas (e.g. 'My behaviour might fail, but I never do') are adaptive. This process greatly reduces the chances of BACKSLIDING when adverse events occur (e.g. the client is criticized by her boss for letting a meeting overrun).

Some clients might see overlearning as 'overdoing it', but this might be due to LOW FRUSTRATION TOLERANCE (exerting minimal effort to effect change), lack of INSIGHT into how new ideas are strengthened or compulsiveness has infiltrated into their overlearning (e.g. 'I must go over these new ideas every day'). Overlearning is a form of investment: the more it is practised now, the more benefits are to be derived from it later.

oversensitivity

This occurs when a client infers that most comments made to or about her are a criticism of her (e.g. 'She asked me to pass the salt rather impatiently I thought. How am I supposed to know she wanted it? What have I done wrong?'). This oversensitivity can occur because, among other reasons, the client believes she is at the centre of everyone else's universe (i.e. they are always talking about her), she cannot discriminate between herself and her behaviour when criticism is levelled at her (see PART–WHOLE ERROR) and her fragile self-esteem predisposes her to scan the environment continuously for signs of disapproval or verbal attack. Why the client turns so many comments into insults or criticisms can usually be traced back to her core beliefs such as 'I'm unlikeable' or 'I'm not good enough'.

Changing general oversensitivity to a proportionate situational sensitivity (i.e. responding to the facts, not incorrect inferences) starts with the client stopping overestimating how critical people are of her, handling actual criticism constructively, and realizing that other people have better and more interesting things to do with their time than always talking about her.

overthinking

Some clients might reply 'I'm still thinking about it' when you ask them if they have made a decision about following a particular course of action. 'Still thinking about it' could indicate overthinking, i.e. endless rumination over making a decision which results in mental paralysis and inaction. Overthinking is often generated by such beliefs as 'I've got to be absolutely certain I've made the right choice. Maybe there's something I've overlooked', 'I must be comfortable with the decision I make' or 'My decision must not backfire in any way.' Help clients to see that balanced and committed thinking involves realizing that:

• Decisions are made on the available information, never all the information as this presupposes one can know what all the information is. Unless the outcome is virtually guaranteed, making decisions involves uncertainty.
• They can feel uncomfortable about the decision without being plagued by agonizing self-doubt and still work hard to achieve a successful outcome.
• If the decision does backfire, this is unfortunate but further decisions will have to be made to reduce the adverse impact of the outcome. A return to overthinking at this point is likely to make matters worse.

Overthinking is often overtaken by events (e.g. the client misses the deadline for the return of the job application form), so this can be another reason for clients to introduce a decision deadline into their thinking. Encouraging clients to take a constructive risk and act on their thoughts (e.g. asking a woman for a date) is another way of helping them to think appropriately rather than to overthink.

overvalued ideas

These are ideas which clients attach too much importance or truth to in the absence of objective evidence to confirm this importance or truth, e.g. a client strongly believes that having malicious thoughts about her friend means she will automatically harm her in some way, even though she has had these thoughts for months and her friend remains unharmed. Overvalued ideation can be viewed as egocentric thinking: 'I think it, therefore it must be true' – the mere presence of the thought authenticates it. The world inside the client's head does not necessarily correspond to the world outside of it: 'If harm is to come to your friend, it is not your thoughts alone that will do it, but you acting on those thoughts. How likely is it that you are going to act on those malicious thoughts and why haven't you acted on them already?'

If thoughts are facts, then half the nation would be wiped out as most people have probably thought at one time or another 'I'll strangle her', or 'I'll kill him'. Looking for the evidential and usefulness basis of the client's overvalued ideas can help her to see they are actually of poor value in terms of accuracy and time spent focused on them.

ownership

In order for clients to take charge of their problems, they need to claim ownership of the thoughts and feelings connected to them (see A–C THINKING and EMOTIONAL RESPONSIBILITY). For example, some clients report their thoughts in an impersonal way such as 'You are stupid if you can't answer a simple question' and 'One would see oneself as a failure in those circumstances'. What these thoughts lack is a personal voice (Neenan and Dryden 2000a). This voice can be gained by encouraging your clients to talk in the first person singular: 'I see myself as stupid if I can't answer a simple question' and 'I'm a failure in those circumstances'.

Similarly, when clients describe their feelings, encourage them to use the active voice (e.g. 'I make myself angry when things don't go right') instead of the passive voice (e.g. 'When things don't go right, this makes me angry'). When ownership is confirmed, clients can then decide what thoughts and feelings to keep, modify or discard.

paradigm shift

This means a fundamental change in a person's outlook. You might make the mistake of being focused solely on finding evidence to disconfirm the client's personal paradigm (e.g. 'I'm unlikeable. I've never had any friends'), thinking that once this evidence has been presented to the client a paradigm shift will naturally occur. However, as DiGiuseppe explains, this is not the case:

> People frequently hold on to beliefs that they know are logically flawed and do not lead to accurate predictions of reality, but no alternative ideas are available to replace the flawed idea. The history of science is filled with such examples. People do not give up ideas, regardless of the evidence against the idea, unless they have an alternative idea to replace it
>
> (DiGiuseppe 1991: 181)

As Padesky (1994) suggests, once a core maladaptive belief has been identified, move as quickly as possible to develop collaboratively an alternative, adaptive belief that the client can focus on and collect evidence for (e.g. 'I would like to see myself as likeable sometimes and able to make a few friends'). Simply chipping away at an old belief can reinforce it (e.g. 'I suppose I'm less worthless than before') while moving towards new and appealing possibilities in the client's life is more likely to induce a paradigm shift.

part–whole error

This error occurs when a person rates herself (e.g. 'I'm useless') on the basis of an aspect of herself (e.g. 'I missed a deadline at work'). This form of reasoning is illogical because the 'self' is made up of many parts, not just the ones the person perceives as bad or defective; therefore, the 'self' can never be defined by a part(s). To get this point across, ask your clients if their feet (part) accurately represent their body (whole) or if they would condemn a house (whole) because of a rusty doorknocker (part) (see OVERGENERALIZING).

passive-aggressiveness

This means someone who dislikes you getting back at you indirectly (e.g. saying 'yes' when he means 'no', spreading malicious rumours about you, suggesting you do things he hopes you will fail at). If you confront the person about his passive-aggressive attitude towards you, he is likely to reply: 'Sounds like you've got the problem. Are you paranoid or something?' While this is a difficult problem to deal with, we suggest some of the following steps:

1. Bring the problem out into the open in a non-confrontational way and invite the person to discuss any interpersonal difficulties he may experience with you.
2. Be open-minded to the possibility that the other person may have a legitimate grievance against you and, if this is the case, express your desire to put the matter right.
3. Frequently summarize the other person's viewpoint, so he feels understood.
4. If both of you agree on what the problem is, then a mutually satisfactory course of action can be drawn up to resolve the problem.

If the person does not want to get involved in this kind of discussion, you can say: 'From my viewpoint, I believe you are acting in a hostile way towards me. I will bring this to your attention from time to time, and each time I do, I will ask you if you wish to discuss it. I will also be keeping detailed notes of your behaviour towards me, so I have some basis for my suspicions.' You might find as you have 'rumbled' him, he might be less inclined to continue his passive-aggressive activities. Living or working with people who have passive-aggressive tendencies towards you can be tough, but not unbearable if you develop an attitude of HIGH FRUSTRATION TOLERANCE.

passivity

Some clients might believe that as passive participants in therapy, they will absorb knowledge from you which will then, without any or little effort on their part, transform their mental landscape and, in a short space of time, they will be thinking, feeling and behaving differently.

Passivity might be appropriate at times in sex or having a massage, but it will not promote therapeutic change. For knowledge to be transformed into personal belief, clients have to work hard to internalize new ideas through HOMEWORK assignments.

With regard to constructing a personal vocabulary of change, clients can remove passivity from it and add: 'Practice, practice, practice!' (Nezu et al. 2001). Would reading a book on chess automatically make clients better players or does this reading need to be coupled with many hours of practice? Reading plus repeated practice also applies to self-help books because clients often 'expect that the knowledge in these books will go into them passively, and that this passive knowledge will make them change. In other words, reading will do the trick without anything else' (Dryden and Gordon 1993a: 129).

past events

Clients often believe that past events cause their present emotional problems (e.g. 'I wasn't loved as a child, so that's why I feel depressed'). The past has an iron grip on the present which clients may view as impossible to free themselves from or they assume they will have to engage in lengthy explorations of the past in order to find 'the cause of it all'. Past events only continue to intrude into the present because of clients' *current* thinking about these events (e.g. 'As I wasn't loved by my parents that meant, and will always mean, that I'm worthless') and the 'cause' is to be found in clients continuing adherence to these past beliefs.

Helping clients to develop adaptive, alternative beliefs (e.g. 'I can accept and nurture myself in spite of my parents lack of love for me. I will stop listening to and believing in those messages from the past') allows them to see that their present and future is likely to be more inviting than their past. Another way to demonstrate that it is not past events per se that cause present problems but the meanings we attach to these events, is to ask clients which unpleasant past events no longer trouble them and which still do; then elicit the reasons for this difference.

'people make me feel . . .'

Like PAST EVENTS, clients frequently believe that other people cause them to feel the way that they do (e.g. 'She made me angry by not going out with me'). This view suggests that feelings are given to us by other people. In order to demonstrate to clients that they largely determine their own feelings, i.e. they give them to themselves, try to 'make' them feel a certain way:

Therapist: I want you to feel happy about her turning you down.
Client: That's silly. I can't feel happy, only angry.
Therapist: If she can make you feel angry, why can't I make you feel happy? I'm giving you feelings in the same way that she does.

The client cannot feel happy because he does not evaluate being turned down as a pleasurable experience; his anger may stem from his belief: 'She thinks I'm not good enough for her. How dare she!' Our feelings are largely determined by how we think about others' comments and actions. Another way to reinforce this point is to find examples when clients resisted others' attempts to make them feel a particular way (e.g. 'My partner tries to make me feel guilty when I eat too much. It never works though because I enjoy my food. If she wants to diet, that's up to her').

perfectionism

If you did an activity perfectly, would you be able to do it again? For example, a gymnast gets a perfect '10' for her performance on the beam, but doing the same performance five minutes later gains a '9.5' from the judges. A perfect performance is a rare and fleeting achievement, so would you judge yourself on something that is rare and fleeting? Clients who have perfectionist tendencies would probably say 'Yes' as they desperately try to reproduce a peak performance in order to reconfirm their self-perfection yet continually fail and lapse into despair and self-laceration.

If such clients would take an overall and realistic view of their performance, they might conclude, for example, that they were competent most of the time, excellent some of the time, failed occasionally, and in rare instances entered, for a very short period, the ethereal realm of perfection. That perfection is so rarely experienced underscores the irrevocable truth of human FALLIBILITY. Paradoxically, those who insist on being perfect often end up with poor results – they reinforce their feared imperfection – because they want to bypass TRIAL AND ERROR in improving their performance and hit the high point straightaway (see Antony and Swinson 1998).

permission-giving beliefs (Beck et al. 1993)

When some clients return to drinking, smoking, drug-taking, gambling, overeating, etc., they may say it just happened 'out of the blue' or 'one thing led to another'. If you carefully retrace the steps that led to the resumption of the particular behaviour, you are likely to find that they gave themselves permission to indulge again, e.g. 'I've been off the booze for six months with no problems. Things are tough at work at the moment and one drink won't hurt. Anyway, I deserve a treat after all my hard work.'

These clients have, in effect, given themselves permission to reactivate their old problems and, if permission follows upon permission, a lapse (stumble) will turn into a relapse (collapse), e.g. 'I've had one drink. I feel good. I'm still in control, so I'll have another one.' Withholding permission will be a struggle for such clients particularly at times of interpersonal strife or when experiencing unpleasant feelings, but this stern stance will help their progress to continue while the justifications in permission giving will undermine it.

persistence

When clients say 'It would be nice if I could be like that' (achieving the desired change), what transforms yearning into actuality is persistence at bringing this change about. We would describe persistence as the unexciting side of therapy – the slog between sessions. Ellis (1984) describes persistence as 'hard work and practice' if clients are to alter their maladaptive beliefs, disturbed feelings and counterproductive behaviours (see MOTIVATION). Persistence requires the development of a philosophy of endurance (e.g. 'Keep on keeping on, whatever it takes'), not just for the short term but also for the long term if clients' therapeutic gains are to be maintained.

Some dictionary definitions of persistence include 'continuing obstinately', which implies behavioural inflexibility or pushing forward unthinkingly. We leave obstinacy out of our discussion of persistence because we want clients to think and act flexibly in the face of changing circumstances as they strive to reach their goals (Neenan and Dryden 2002).

If some clients decide that sustained effort is too hard to bear and quit therapy, their persistence at not persisting is likely to create more problems for them. The original and now additional problems will require more persistence (persistence plus) in tackling them if clients are not to be overwhelmed by these problems. When clients shudder at the thought of persistence, remind them that the consequences of not persevering with change are likely to be worse than tolerating the uncomfortable struggle of 'sticking with it'. Persistence, properly applied, usually pays off (see QUICK FIX).

personal domain

This is whatever a person considers to be important in his life (e.g. having close friends, a good job, a loving partner, his moral code).

Looking out from his domain, the 'person's emotional response - or emotional disturbance - depends on whether he perceives events as adding to, subtracting from, endangering, or impinging upon his domain' (Beck 1976: 56). We might say that the personal domain is the sun around which planets orbit. These planets contain the THEMES (italicized in the forthcoming examples) that may affect his personal domain depending on how he appraises the events that happen on these planets. For example, the person feels depressed by the end of a close friendship because he appraises this *loss* as a significant subtraction from his domain, he becomes anxious when he thinks about the *threat* of showing how nervous he is when speaking to a large group as he believes this will endanger his domain, and he feels joy when he becomes head of department at work because this is an *expansion* of his domain. To discover why a person reacts in the way that he does to events in his life, CBT aims to understand both his personal domain and his idiosyncratic interpretation of events within this domain (Wills and Sanders 1997).

personal scientist

This refers to individuals being able 'to pose and test hypotheses, as do scientists, and to acquire their information by experimentation' (Wessler 1986: 6). From the CBT viewpoint, distressed clients have become poor scientists because they are not testing effectively their hypotheses (e.g. 'I'm a failure') and thereby reaffirming their distorted view of themselves or reality. However, some clients might feel intimidated (e.g. 'I haven't got the brains for it') or bewildered (e.g. 'Am I supposed to wear a white coat or something?') by the concept of becoming a personal scientist. To allay such worries, explain to clients that therapy is just an extension of what they do already - testing things out:

> You test the bathwater before putting the baby into it; take a white knuckle ride at the fair to see if you can cope with it; go out with someone to determine if you are compatible with them; experiment with recipes in order to become a better cook . . . and so on. Now, with your current problems, you need to test out some of your thoughts and beliefs to see if they fit the facts or, if they don't, maybe different conclusions are called for.

CBT hopes to make clients into better personal scientists not only for present problem-solving but also for any future challenge they are presented with, e.g. 'My boss wants me to run a seminar. Can I do it? How do I find out if I can?' (To help your clients develop their skills as a personal scientist, see Strohmer and Blustein 1990.)

personalization

This occurs when clients assume responsibility for events outside of their control (e.g. 'My wife can't seem to maintain any friendships, so it must be my fault'). Personalization often results in guilt. Encourage your clients to depersonalize (make impersonal) such events in order to foster objectivity. Burns suggests that clients have

> confused *influence* with *control* over others . . . you will certainly influence the people you interact with, but no one could reasonably expect you to control them. What the other person does is ultimately his or her responsibility, not yours.
>
> (Burns 1981: 39; original author's italics)

In the above example, the client tries to influence his wife to 'initiate more things. You can't expect everybody to keep running to you', but no longer believes it is his fault if she does not heed his advice or cannot maintain friendships.

phoniness

Phoniness is pretending to be something one is not. When clients worry about being, or believe they have been, revealed as a 'phoney', they are mistaken in this belief. Their so-called phoniness does not stem from their attempts to be what they are not, but from their unrealistic standards and personae they have created for themselves (e.g. 'I must never let my friends down and if I do, this means I'm a false friend'; 'I must be master of my subject and if I can't answer a question, then I will be seen as a pretender, no longer pre-eminent'). You can show your clients that their 'phoniness' is produced by their rigid MUSTS and refusal to accept their FALLIBILITY. In addition, maintaining such personae takes lots of energy and can eventually lead to emotional exhaustion.

When clients are undergoing change, they can see themselves as 'phoneys' because of the unnaturalness of their new thoughts and behaviours (see 'FEELING STRANGE'). Helping clients through this difficult phase is facilitated by pointing out

> the difference between *pretending* and *practicing* . . . People are pretending, or acting in a phony fashion, when they do not have a sincere desire to bring about permanent change and only go through the motions of changing. People are practicing, or behaving genuinely, when they diligently try to learn something new with a sincere desire to change.
>
> (Grieger and Boyd 1980: 165; original authors' italics)

Acting differently indicates newness, not phoniness. Hauck (1982b) suggests that what clients regard as phoney behaviour is nothing more than breaking in a new pair of shoes.

positive thinking

Some clients might believe that positive thinking is the antidote to negative thinking. However, positive thinking has the same drawbacks as negative thinking: it is often inaccurate and self-defeating. For example, a client keeps telling himself 'to think positively and everything will be all right', but his problems are actually getting worse because of his inattention to tackling them. Between positive and negative thinking, there is realistic thinking which relies on '*gathering accurate information to pinpoint and counteract distortions*' (Beck et al. 1979: 299; original authors' italics). Tempering optimism with realism helps clients to see that not every cloud has a silver lining; some of them might be storm clouds ahead, so they need to keep a weather eye open and an action plan handy.

power struggle

If you allow yourself to be drawn into a power struggle, this may be because you believe your ego is on the line: you have to dominate to prove you are a competent therapist and 'I know best'. As well as wasting valuable therapy time, power struggles involve winners and losers – therapy as a tug-of-war. We suggest you let go of your end of the rope (Walen et al. 1992). Tell your argumentative or recalcitrant client that your ego is not on the line and if she fails to make progress or do any therapeutic work, you will not suffer. If she thinks she has 'won' because you have thrown in the towel, inform her that she has also 'lost' (i.e. she is still stuck with her emotional problems – a pyrrhic victory). Therefore, what to do next is her choice: stay and work or leave and come back when she is in the right frame of mind (Neenan and Dryden 2000b).

pre-emptive strike

In other words, do it to them before they can do it to us. For example, a person might say to her partner that they do not go out enough, but before she can continue, he angrily retorts: 'We could go out more if you brought in some more money, so pull your financial weight in this house before you start lecturing me about going out more.' If he had not interrupted her, he might have felt stung by the criticism and concluded that she was accusing him of being 'a stay-at-home bore'. The pre-emptive strike forestalled such uncomfortable self-reflection. As Beck observes:

> While it is true that the preemptive strike may temporarily spare you some pain, it will ultimately cause more pain as a result of the continued, unpleasant encounters with your spouse and the ill-effects of the unsolved problem.
>
> (Beck 1989: 135)

Learning to listen to criticism and carefully consider its validity can help the person to dispense with pre-emptive strikes and improve communication with his partner.

prejudice

Clients' negative core beliefs about themselves (e.g. 'I'm no good') can be likened to self-prejudice (Padesky 1993a). Prejudice refers to 'those beliefs – whether right or wrong – which are either formed prior to proper consideration of the evidence or else maintained in defiance of it' (Flew 1975: 29). Padesky (1994) suggests clients can be asked to nominate a person who holds a prejudice they do not agree with (e.g. 'Women are not as capable as men in top management jobs') and then use this person's prejudice as a frame of reference to understand their own: 'When women do succeed at that level he dismisses it as a fluke. He just won't have it. I suppose it's like me: when people tell me of the good things I do, I try to discount what they say in order to confirm in my mind that I'm still no good.'

Clients might hold beliefs that are positively-toned (e.g. 'I always give everybody the benefit of the doubt') but they are still prejudiced beliefs because the EVIDENCE (e.g. the client has been 'ripped off' several times) has not been properly considered – wariness might be appropriate with some individuals. Combating prejudice leads to more OPEN-MINDEDNESS but do not expect your clients (or yourself) to be able or inclined to surrender every prejudice because a few have been.

preview experience (Knaus 1998)

This means, on one occasion, acting in the way the person wants to act, e.g. instead of spending months avoiding going to the gym, she finally attends and enjoys the workout. Whether the preview experience remains a one-off or a precursor to sustained change, depends on her commitment to overcoming her PROCRASTINATION.

problem-solving

Solving personal problems is a basic life skill (Brammer 1990). Some clients might baulk at the effort required of them to learn a model of effective problem-solving (e.g. D'Zurilla 1990; McKay et al. 1997; Wasik 1984). Looking at the complex steps involved, clients might ask: 'Do I really have to do all that?' (McKay et al. 1997: 174), to which you might reply:

> Problem maintenance is relatively effortless. I don't need to teach you how to keep your problems going as you seem able to do that yourself. On the other hand, effective problem-solving is hard work. I do need to teach you how to use a particular model. Once you've grasped how the model works and see some positive results from it, you can ask yourself if you want to continue 'to do all that' or return to the relative ease of problem mainte-nance.

For clients with longstanding maladaptive problem-solving styles, it is important to remind them that several sessions of problem-solving training will not produce much of a difference in their life (Heppner 1990). Therefore, PERSISTENCE in problem-solving is required.

procrastination

Procrastination is often referred to as 'the thief of time'. This is incor-rect: when a person procrastinates he steals his own time through his continuing inaction. Another view of procrastination is that the person gives away his time free of charge – time that he might pay anything for on his deathbed in order to stay alive a little longer. A person can waste so much time procrastinating that it may seem to her that she has several lives to lead instead of only one. People who become upset with their procrastination habits see themselves as wasting their lives yet avoid doing what would help them to make productive use of their time. This is what Knaus (1998) calls the procrastination paradox. Clients often prolong their procrastination in therapy by spending too much time ventilating their feelings (e.g. 'I feel angry with myself for continually putting off finishing these projects') instead of devising an anti-procrastination plan.

Whatever the person's justification or rationalization for procrasti-nating, overcoming it 'requires *work*, and typically lots of it. Ironic as it may seem, the problem of avoiding work can only be solved by doing *more work*' (Knaus 1993, section II: 37; original author's italics). Moreover, work on a lifelong basis to break the procrastination habit, not just to overcome a present bout of inaction. With this outlook, the person gradually sees herself as a 'doer' instead of a 'stewer'. If time is our most precious resource, then procrastination gives the lie to it.

progress plateau

After some improvement, a client might become 'stuck', i.e. further improvement is proving elusive. Stranded on a progress plateau might occur because the client, among other reasons, is not prepared to expend any further effort on problem-solving, believes that progress is self-perpetuating after an initial 'nudge' from him, discounts what progress has already been made because he keeps moving the goalposts, has not considered objectively his LIMITATIONS, has an ideal goal in his sights rather than the ostensible one you believe he is working on or he feels compelled to push for further progress at the insistence of others but his heart is no longer in it. Whether clients decide to leave therapy satisfied with their current progress, push on with the same or revised goals, the reasons for this decision need to be realistic, honest and open instead of self-defeating (see REVIEWING PROGRESS).

(six) 'P's

The six 'P's represent a capsule account of the development, maintenance and amelioration of emotional disorders. The six 'P's are:

1. *Problem* – what is the client's current difficulty (e.g. depression)?
2. *Precipitant* – what triggered the depression (e.g. end of a relationship)?
3. *Predisposition* – what factors made it likely the client would develop depression (e.g., he could only feel safe and happy within a relationship: 'When I feel I'm wanted, that means everything to me.')?
4. *Perpetuation* – how is the problem being maintained (e.g. withdrawal and inactivity coupled with a bleak view of the present and future)?
5. *Promotion* – how is constructive change to be effected (e.g. through a multimodal problem-solving plan such as activity scheduling and examining and changing the client's depressogenic thinking)?
6. *Persistence* – how is the change process to be maintained including coping with setbacks (e.g. through repeated practice of the client's new problem-solving skills)?

Good therapy involves a balanced consideration of all six 'P's' and when therapy stalls, it may be due to you neglecting a 'P' or spending too much time on a 'P'. So watch your 'P's' as well as your 'Q's!

put-downs

When a client says she is very upset about someone putting her down (e.g. 'This bloke I met said he wouldn't sleep with me unless I put a bag over my head'), you can ask: 'Who ultimately put you down: him or you?' Did the client agree with the put-down, reflect on its validity or dismiss it along with him? The client agreed with the put-down because she had a low opinion of herself and her looks and was always seeking approval from men (which she rarely got). In order not to unduly upset herself over offensive remarks (put up with put-downs), the client learnt to moderate her approval needs through self- and facial acceptance and started verbal sparring instead of emotionally over-reacting when experiencing put-downs (e.g. 'Let me put it like this: I'll put a bag over my head if you put one over yours').

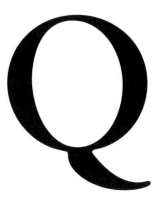

quandary

A person might be faced with a choice between two equally desirable alternatives (e.g. she has to choose which man to go out with when she finds them both equally attractive). She might believe 'I want them both' but realizes she had better make a decision soon otherwise she might lose both of them to other women or because of their own impatience for a decision from her. In order for her quandary not to become a period of prolonged indecision, she needs to realize that enjoying one desirable alternative is better than missing out on both, that she has not 'lost' the pleasure of the alternative relationship because she is not going to experience it (she cannot lose what she never had), and continually regretting her inability to exercise her other choice may result in her enjoying less the relationship she does eventually embark on (see DILEMMA).

quart into a pint pot

This refers to individuals who try to get too much out of life and eventually experience self-defeating consequences. These individuals may be driven by such beliefs as these: 'Every minute has to be maximized'; 'I must continually prove my worth by taking on more and more tasks'; 'I mustn't miss out on any opportunity'; 'I can't stand any idleness or boredom in my life.' These beliefs and the behaviours that flow from them often result in psychological overload: the individual suffers a severe stress reaction or worse resulting in diminished capacity and functioning. The problem now is even filling the pint pot, let alone trying to get more into it.

Leading a full, but not impossibly full, life includes:

- developing a flexible outlook such as setting aside non-striving, relaxing time.
- learning to be oneself instead of continually trying to prove oneself without lowering one's personal standards.
- accepting that the only way to make use of every opportunity is to clone oneself!
- tolerating unavoidable periods of idleness and boredom without accompanying disturbance-inducing visions of precious time wasted and life unfulfilled.

questions (rhetorical)

Rhetorical questions imply their own answers rather than seek information. For example, when talking about her problems, a client might say, 'Why do these things keep happening to me?' (possible answer: 'They shouldn't keep happening to me. I can't stand it!') and 'Is she my friend or what?' (possible answer: 'She's a bitch for letting me down!'). Clients can become irritated if you keep on asking them to turn their questions into clear statements, but you can point out that rhetorical questions are often tied to strong affect and contain maladaptive ideas that they may not be aware of (Grieger and Boyd 1980).

Making clear what is implied reduces the potential for confusion and reveals what disturbed thoughts and feelings need to addressed. In the above example, the client was able to reveal an underlying assumption – 'When I want my friends' help, they should always be there for me' – which led to her feeling angry and hurt when they were not there for her (this is what she meant by 'These things keep happening to me') and finding yet another 'false' friend.

quick fix

Everyone has probably had a quick fix or two at some time in their life. When quick fixes become a habitual response to stressful events, then the person is likely to develop longer-term problems (e.g. taking tranquillizers to quell bouts of anxiety develops into dependence on the tablets, but the causes of the anxiety remain unaddressed). What does a quick fix actually fix? It might provide relief in the short term but it also fixes (i.e. keeps securely in place) the underlying problem. The more quick fixes the person pursues, the greater the fix he gets himself into. Quick fixes are often likened to sticking plasters, so the next time a client wants a quick fix, mention to him that he is already covered with them, and then suggest: 'They clearly haven't worked, so why reproduce in therapy something that isn't working for you? How about considering an enduring solution to your problems?'

quitting therapy

When some of your clients announce they are quitting therapy after a couple of sessions, find out why success has occurred so quickly or disillusionment has set in so early. With the former, ask your clients what accounts for this rapid change: are they thinking and acting differently so they no longer upset themselves over their problems? (Ask for examples of this cognitive and behavioural shift.) Has the situation changed but not their thinking about it? If this is the case, their disturbance-inducing thinking remains intact and ready to be reactivated if the situation(s) becomes aversive again. The appearance of success may not lead to sustained success if premature termination is based on avoiding addressing the central factors maintaining clients' difficulties.

With regard to the latter problem of clients' disillusionment, this may involve some of the following reasons: misunderstanding what COMMITMENT means in the change process, expecting that there should be a quick fix available, believing that change can occur without hard work or the experience of emotional discomfort, and/or assuming that change cannot occur without MOTIVATION. Discussing these reasons and tackling the fallacies underpinning them may encourage some clients to stay in therapy and 'soldier on'.

quitting vs. cutting down

This refers to abstinence versus controlled use of substances (e.g. drink, drugs) as the goal for change. Clients are unlikely to choose a goal to which they are not committed. You might keep on pushing for abstinence when the client still believes, probably erroneously, that he can control his drinking despite many failed attempts to do so. You can suggest as a compromise one more attempt at controlled drinking and, if this fails as it is likely to do, the clinical focus can switch to abstinence. Goals can be 'renegotiated if data gathered during therapy support a change' (Ellis et al. 1988: 48). Abstinence can then become the self-control strategy. A detailed cost-benefit analysis can help the client to be more committed to this new goal.

Problem drinkers (i.e. non-severe alcohol problems), whose aim is controlled drinking, and who insist that this is a realistic goal, might be persuaded, in some cases, to experiment with a period of abstinence (e.g. six months) followed by a gradual return to controlled consumption.

The results from this experiment can provide compelling evidence (e.g. many lapses during the abstinence period) whether controlled drinking is really attainable for a particular problem drinker. To learn to drink moderately or never to drink again, that is the question, but it often takes a long time before it is successfully and honestly answered by the client.

rating

If clients play the 'rating game', then it is important for them to learn what can be realistically and objectively rated – such as a behaviour or trait – and what cannot be – themselves. For example, a client might conclude that, on the basis of a poor performance, she is incompetent. As Leahy notes: 'Performance is a measure of a behavior, not a person. Are you assuming that your specific behavior in this specific situation is a measure of your value as a person?' (1996: 101). In order to rate what can be accurately rated, semantic precision is required, e.g. 'I failed my driving test, but I'm not a failure as a person. In order to be a failure as a person, I would have to fail at every single thing I have done, am doing and will do.' Rating what can be legitimately rated helps clients to improve their performance and learn from their mistakes while rating themselves usually leads to self-condemnation and stagnation in PROBLEM-SOLVING.

rational barb (Kimmel 1976)

When clients are at a loss about how to deal with hurtful criticism or PUT-DOWNS, they can learn to emasculate such comments through rational barbs. Barbs are only as powerful and as hurtful as clients allow them to be, so 'debarbing' starts with clients pinpointing why such comments 'strike home' (e.g. 'It's true. I am a fat bastard') and learning to develop a more compassionate self-appraisal (e.g. 'I am overweight which I want to do something about, but being hard on myself just increases the load I have to carry'). With their permission, you can call clients hurtful names (barbs) and they can practise responding with coping statements without emotional disturbance intruding (e.g. 'By "fat bastard", I presume you mean I have my weight problem to deal with and you have your malicious mind to keep you company. I am unhappy with my weight at times, but I'd be far unhappier if I had to live in a mind like yours').

rational correctness

CBT teaches clients that their emotional problems can be modified by improving their use of REASON and REALITY TESTING as part of their developing role as a self-therapist. Once formal therapy has ended, some clients might believe erroneously that they must be rational at all times: 'There is only one way to think about things otherwise my time in therapy will have been wasted'; hence their adherence to rational correctness.

This statement shows that the client still has some blind spots in his thinking: he did not absorb the lessons of RELAPSE PREVENTION (i.e. setbacks are likely); that human FALLIBILITY cannot be removed through rational thinking; that reason will not banish emotional distress from his life; and he is not paying attention to the evidence that undermines rational correctness – he has become disturbed again! Thinking more rationally will help clients to reduce the intensity, frequency and duration of their future problems; demanding that they must always be rational is likely to have the opposite effect on these problems (see EMOTIONAL CORRECTNESS).

rationality

As with IRRATIONALITY, our view of rationality is straightforward: adopting beliefs and actions that will help the client to reach her desired and realistic goals. For example, a client who believes 'I very much want to lose two stone but I don't have to lose it in order to be happy or accept myself' diets and exercises non-compulsively in order to achieve her goal. Setbacks along the way (e.g. breaking her diet, failing to exercise) are not turned into self-disturbances as the client sees setbacks as part of the change process. Being rational also involves long-term thinking: if the client wants to maintain her new weight, then continuing EFFORT is required from her. Rationality is based on flexible thinking, so alternative plans are available if desired goals are not realized. Unlike clients who hold irrational beliefs, clients who subscribe to rational beliefs would usually want others (e.g. children, partner, friends) to adopt these beliefs because they realize how self-helping they are.

'rationality isn't everything' (Hauck 1980a)

When clients learn (and accept) that they are largely responsible for their own emotional reactions to events, some of them might assume that they can behave less courteously or caringly to others because 'If they get upset, that's their responsibility, not mine'. While this statement is true, such clients distort the lessons of therapy: becoming more emotionally resilient is not at the expense of deliberately provoking, hurting or abusing others, or being indifferent to their feelings. Rational thinking is used for self-improvement, not to expose the sensitivities of others. For example, a client tells his friend that his haircut is 'hideous and it makes you look like a moron' when a bland 'it's OK' would not have caused offence. The client's vital interests were not threatened in any way, so his 'always tell it as I see it' approach is both impolite and unnecessary.

rationalization

When clients engage in rationalization they are maintaining their problems rather than tackling them successfully. For example, a person who is turned down for a job she desperately wanted might say, 'I didn't want it anyway.' If she was to admit honestly, in the light of her unsuccessful job application, how much she actually wanted the job she might conclude: 'I'm no good. You're nothing without a job.' Rationalization helps her to avoid painful self-reflection and consequent self-judgement.

Adopting rational thinking instead of rationalizing allows the person to see that no one has to give her a job, no matter how desperately she wants one; so PERSISTENCE and learning from interview errors is required from her. She now realizes that tying her self-worth to having a job means she will be depressed without one and anxious when she gets one as she will continually worry about losing it; therefore, self-worth should have no strings attached to it. We acknowledge, and it is important to point this out to your clients, that rational thinking is usually hard won, 'whereas rationalization often comes easily to someone who is acting defensively' (Feltham and Dryden 1993: 154).

raw data

Clients provide raw data in the form of their thoughts and feelings about events in their life. Clients usually believe that this information is an accurate description of these events. However, these data often contain 'crooked' thinking such as inaccurate inferences (e.g. 'I'll never recover from this setback') and maladaptive conclusions (e.g. 'This set-back proves I'm incompetent'). Processing these raw data is based on SCIENTIFIC THINKING whereby clients are encouraged to look for evidence to validate or falsify their inferences and conclusions. Adopting this method of thinking allows the client to discover, as in the above example,

that setbacks are temporary, not permanent, and that specific perfor-
mances or actions can be described as 'incompetent' but such labels are
inaccurate and meaningless when applied to the person. We might say
that the raw data have been sufficiently 'cooked' (processed) when
clients are able to view events in an objective and undisturbed way.

'real me'

Some clients, when going through troubled and unhappy times, say
they want to find or reclaim the 'real me'. The 'real me' usually refers to
a pristine and authentic self buried beneath the rubble of their present
troubles or concealed by the false self 'imposed' upon them by the
pressures of modern life and the expectations of others. Once the 'real
me', estranged from the current self, is discovered, then happiness,
harmony and simplicity will return to the person's life. We believe the
'real me' is a myth. As Appleyard says, writing about celebrities in
torment and in search of their authentic self,

> . . . there is no 'real self', no 'child within', no 'real me', no authentic essence
> somehow concealed beneath some malign combination of drugs, sex, fame
> and money. There are only people who live and people who just talk about
> it.
>
> (Appleyard 2001: 2)

The self is complex and ever-changing and cannot be pinned down to a
few eternal attributes or fixed in time when 'I really knew who I was'.
The 'real me' encompasses anything that happens in the person's life –
the good, the bad and the indifferent – and the question the person
needs to ask herself is this: does she want to find effective and enduring
solutions to her current problems or embark on a futile search for an
unlocatable place where an unproven concept apparently exists?

reality-testing

Do not let therapy become a clash between competing views of reality
(yours vs. your client's) – let the data do the talking! As Beck et al.
comment:

> The therapist can say he does not know whether things are or are not as bad
> as the patient paints them, but that he wants to check the facts and see . . .
> The major premise in cognitive therapy is to speak from the data – not
> attempt to convince the patient through force of argument.
>
> (Beck et al. 1979: 300)

Treat the client's thoughts as hypotheses which then require reality-testing to determine if the resulting data fit the facts as the client sees them or if there are other explanations which seem more plausible (i.e. fit the facts better). Agreeing on an experiment to test the client's belief reinforces the vital principle and practice of collaboration thereby reducing potential RESISTANCE (Alford and Beck 1997). Trying to persuade the client of the correctness of your view of reality undermines the concept that therapy is based on OPEN-MINDEDNESS.

reason

We use reason in two ways: first, in order to change, clients need to have a reason to change; and second, they need to use their reason to change (Dryden 2001). Finding a reason to change is usually much easier for clients than using their reason to change. For example, a client wants to overcome her social anxiety in order to enjoy a fuller life, but, so far, reason has not proved helpful. We all use reason, but not equally well; so therapy is not teaching clients how to reason but to discover how they are using reason with regard to their problems, e.g. how do they evaluate EVIDENCE and draw conclusions? By learning to think clearly and critically, clients can reason better in order to realize their desired changes.

reassurance

Providing reassurance to clients who are reassurable can be helpful, but providing it to clients who cannot be reassured becomes part of the problem, not the solution. For example, continually reassuring a client who believes she has a brain tumour, despite medical evidence to the contrary, can reinforce in her mind that something is indeed wrong: 'If I was fine, then why all this reassurance? I wonder what he [GP] is not telling me.' One way of demonstrating the ineffectiveness of reassurance-seeking is to ask clients how much reassurance they would need from you in order to have 'peace of mind' for the next six or twelve months? (Salkovskis and Bass 1997). Clients readily concede that no matter how much reassurance they received, it would not last more than a day or two, let alone six or twelve months.

When clients are reassured (usually temporarily), what does this say about the cause of their symptoms? As Wells observes, questions that can reinforce a psychological explanation of the problem include: 'If reassurance makes you feel better, would that work if you are seriously ill?', 'Is reassurance a cure for . . . (e.g. cancer, heart disease)?' and

'Would a serious illness respond to reassurance in this way?' (1997: 145).

Reassurance-seeking does not provide any new answers, just the same replies that clients remained unconvinced by. Therefore, withholding reassurance is not a sadistic treatment strategy, but allows alternative explanations to emerge through discussion and experiment that better explain the client's present symptoms: namely, that it is excessive anxiety about her health, not the presence of a brain tumour, that is maintaining her symptoms. Additionally, if the client accepts the fact that it is impossible to be completely certain that a serious illness will not befall her, then her reassurance-seeking is likely to reduce.

reattribution

Reattribution helps clients to step back and look at the many contributions to an adverse outcome. Thus, a client who blames herself for causing a bad outcome can be helped to see that she cannot be responsible for all the factors that led to this outcome. For example, a client says, 'It is all my fault that my son is unhappy with his marriage.' It is her fault because 'I didn't bring my son up in the right way that would have avoided such unhappiness for him'. This statement reflects the client's godlike assumption of omnipotence, i.e. she has the power to control her son's destiny (see GUILT).

By listing as many factors as possible that have contributed to her son's current unhappiness (e.g. being out of work, constant rows with his wife, noisy neighbours, being in debt, making bad decisions), the client eventually realized that her ability to influence, let alone control, her son's life was severely limited. If she was able to control her son's destiny, then happiness, not unhappiness, would fill his life. Reattribution is not meant to let clients 'off the hook', but to assess accurately their level of responsibility commensurate to producing a particular outcome.

re-education

This means that therapy provides clients with a re-education in emotional causation, i.e. instead of blaming others or events for how they feel, clients' attention is turned inwards to understand the role of distorted thinking and maladaptive beliefs in largely determining their feelings (though environmental contributions to the development of these feelings are not ignored). As Burns (1981) says: you feel as you think. Some clients might complain that they feel like they are back at school or are too old to 'learn new tricks'. You can respond that they probably have had many re-educations in their life and therapy is just the latest one.

Prior re-educations include not believing any longer in certain myths (e.g. your first love is your only true love in life) and superstitions (e.g. walking under ladders brings bad luck), changing political beliefs, realizing that endless bed-hopping or the relentless pursuit of material success can prove ultimately hollow, recognizing belatedly the value of a good education and re-entering the educational system at a mature age, acknowledging that there are more important things in life than long hours at the office. Whether CBT will turn out to be a re-education that clients value can only be determined by them staying in therapy on a 'suck it and see' basis.

rehearsal

In-session rehearsal provides clients with opportunities to test out and improve on new behaviours and skills before they are carried out *in vivo*. Some clients might want to get 'on with it' without any or inadequate rehearsal. With these clients, ask them to imagine the first night of a play with themselves as the actors, but who have not bothered to rehearse. Clients usually reply that they would not want a 'flop' on their hands and rehearsal now makes more sense. Also, rehearsal uncovers obstacles to carrying out the behaviours in real life that can be tackled in the safety of the session. This is preferable to these obstacles being revealed at the next homework review when clients report their failure to execute these behaviours.

rejection

Hauck suggests that 'it is when we reject *ourselves* that we get into emotional trouble, not when others reject us' (1981: 8; original author's emphasis). This may come as a surprise or shock to some clients, but if they carefully analyse the personal MEANING they attach to rejection (e.g. 'Without her, I'm worthless' or 'As he's dumped me, this means I'm physically and sexually repulsive'), this is more likely to account for their painful feelings than the act of rejection itself. Would the emotional pain be as intense if self-rejection was not part of the client's view of events?

Some clients might argue that if they were not worthless, then they would not be rejected, but as they have been rejected, then that proves they are worthless. The only thing this circular argument proves is the absence of clear thinking. When a client is rejected, this means the other person has lost interest in him for whatever reason; if he chooses to make his self-worth contingent upon being loved or wanted, then he is likely to devalue himself when these conditions are absent from his life. No one else can make the client reject or devalue himself; only he can do that.

relapse prevention

Relapse prevention assumes that humans have a natural tendency to slip back into their self-defeating patterns of thinking, feeling and behaving rather than maintaining their progress unwaveringly. Relapse prevention counters some clients' false beliefs that their post-therapy progress will be smooth and uneventful and being a self-therapist was only limited to formal therapy instead of needing to become a way of life (Beck et al. 1993). Maintaining therapeutic gains is often hard work, so adopting an outlook of HIGH FRUSTRATION TOLERANCE supports this maintenance work and guards against 'OSTRICH' THINKING such as only seeing the pleasurable aspects of a situation rather than its potential for relapse – 'I would love to go to that party, but I realize I still crave the drugs, so I'd better keep out of harm's way.' Relapse prevention teaches clients that their progress can never look after itself.

reliving

Sitting in the safety of your office and feeling relatively relaxed can make it difficult for clients to identify their situation-specific 'hot' (emotionally charged) thoughts. One reason for this difficulty is

> . . . state-dependent memory: patients are more likely to retrieve memories when they are experiencing the emotions congruent with those memories: for example, negative memories when depressed.
>
> (Weishaar 1993: 91)

Using imagery can help clients to relive past situations in order to activate affect and associated 'hot' thoughts. For example, a client who said he was unsure why he felt so angry and depressed over his son's comment, 'You're no father to me', was asked to describe the situation in the present tense. By reliving the situation in this way, the client was able to pinpoint the thoughts that led to his distress: 'My whole life is built around my son and he destroyed that life. He pushed me away, humiliated me. I can never forgive him for doing that.'

Reliving past experiences helps to give the lie to clients' and others' complaints that CBT is purely intellectual and therefore pays no attention to understanding or exploring feelings.

resignation

Resignation means reconciling oneself to the inevitable (e.g. 'I'll never be happy') or giving up (e.g. hope). When clients claim to have resigned themselves to a situation or outcome, you need to help them assess whether the facts really support their conclusions. For example, a client who failed to get into Oxford University stated, 'I've resigned myself to the fact that I'm second-rate.' Not getting into Oxford is a genuine fact; calling himself 'second-rate' is a spurious one. He will only know if he was second-rate on his deathbed. Until that time, he has ample opportunity to strive for excellence in his life. Resignation means he will give up this opportunity because of a setback instead of testing his abilities over the long-term.

Resignation can also occur if clients set themselves unrealistic goals (e.g. 'I can never love another woman, so I have to get my partner back or my life will be meaningless'). In this example, the client could love another woman if he was prepared to look beyond his ex-partner and expand his definition of what makes life meaningful.

resistance

Leahy defines resistance as 'anything in the patient's behavior, thinking, affective response, and interpersonal style that interferes with the ability of that patient to utilize the treatment and to acquire the ability to handle problems outside of therapy and after therapy has been terminated' (2001: 11). The starting point for tackling resistance is to ask yourself what the client is resisting, e.g. you, being in therapy, the therapeutic approach, your arguments? From the client's viewpoint, there are usually logical reasons why he is resisting (e.g. changing a maladaptive belief might undermine other beliefs and values he holds dear – see Rorer 1999; the client is only in therapy at someone else's insistence); so do not equate resistance with bloody-mindedness. Also, you should expect some normal resistance if, for example, clients believe their cognitive system is being forced to change too quickly (Dowd 1996), their identity is under threat or that your views of their problems seem far-fetched.

Resistance provides useful information indicating that clients have reservations about or objections to therapy that you need to address (e.g. 'Why do you keep bringing the focus back to me when it's my boss who is the problem in my life? You're looking in the wrong direction'). Resistance often occurs with clients who value autonomy and believe that therapy is trying to deprive them of independence and choice, so presenting options to these clients is very important to maintain their sense of self-direction and control in therapy. Clients with a sociotropic personality style might be afraid to become their own therapist and, instead, seek to develop a dependent relationship with you. Suggesting small experiments to test their fears of 'striking out alone' can help to prevent such an attachment forming.

Whatever the source of clients' resistance, point out to them that if their resistance continues, they will ultimately resist improving their own well-being and thereby perpetuate the very problems they ostensibly wanted to change.

'Client resistance' is the handy label therapists often use when clients do not make progress or terminate therapy prematurely; handy because it avoids reflection on their clinical practice and personal behaviour in therapy. You might not accept the client for being resistant and thereby make therapy harder for him than you would do for a client you got on with; therefore, do not be surprised if the 'resistant' client does not return to therapy.

Other therapist-induced resistances include pushing the client to accept your ambitious goals for change instead of letting him choose his own more modest goals or subscribing to such beliefs as 'My clients must work as hard as I am doing' or 'I must have the approval of my clients' (Ellis 1985). With the latter belief, you might avoid tackling difficult issues with your client because you fear losing his approval thereby leaving these issues intact and ready for reactivation when the client experiences future episodes of emotional strain.

We would suggest that resistance needs to be tackled in a climate of acceptance: of yourself and your client. Keep your ego out of the counselling room, develop a philosophy of HIGH FRUSTRATION TOLERANCE, open-mindedly look for the sources of and reasons for resistance and seek productive ways of dealing with it. Then the issue of resistance might produce less of a heart-sink reaction in you (see Leahy 2001 for a detailed account of overcoming resistance in CBT).

responsibility

Responsibility in CBT does not mean blaming clients for their thoughts, feelings and behaviours, but simply states that these reactions to events belong to them and no one else (see EMOTIONAL RESPONSIBILITY). However, some clients might disclaim responsibility because they believe they have no choice in how they respond to events ('He/she/it makes me feel this way'). For clients to take responsibility for their problems, it is crucial that they see they have the ability to respond differently to events (e.g. being stuck in a long queue can result in anger, annoyance or calmness depending on how the situation is evaluated by the client). Helping clients to develop alternative viewpoints in addressing their problems or pointing out the choices they already have but dismiss, can begin to nurture personal responsibility (e.g. 'I suppose I could control my temper if I'm stuck in a long queue but why should I?').

Sometimes clients reject responsibility because they see no easy options to choose from (e.g. 'I'm not working that bloody hard to change. Stuff it!'). It may come as a surprise to many clients that, as Glover points out, how much choice is available to us:

> We are never, while alive and aware, *quite* deprived of all choice, and in most situations the range of choice is normally greatly in excess of that which we readily acknowledge.
>
> (Glover 1988: 108; original author's emphasis)

Responsibility also involves accepting one's LIMITATIONS: what a person *can* control (his own actions and reactions) and what he *cannot* (other people, events) though he may be able to influence or contribute to these things (e.g. 'I contribute to your depression by ending the relationship, but do not cause it. That's within your power, not mine'). When a client takes responsibility for his actions he also makes himself accountable for them (e.g. 'I knew I shouldn't have taken the drugs, but I did. So that's why I relapsed') and can also choose to learn from his actions and mistakes instead of repeating them (see LEARNING). Responsibility can be a liberating message for clients because

> . . . it states that you can change how you feel by changing the beliefs that you hold. You don't have to rely on changing others or situations first, which, if this was the case, would make personal change very much more difficult.
>
> (Dryden 2001: 15)

reviewing progress

Assuming your client is making progress is not the same as conducting a formal review of progress. Such reviews will help you to determine:

1. whether your client is actually making progress on his target problem;
2. if your 'sense' of his progress is confirmed by his assessment of his progress;

3. whether there are obstacles blocking his progress (e.g. ambivalence about change);
4. if a change in goal direction is required (e.g. the initial goal now seems too ambitious);
5. how your client measures his progress (e.g. in absolute or relative terms);
6. the basis of the client's change (e.g. is he facing his fears or distracting himself from them?);
7. a suitable time for termination (e.g. 'On the basis of our progress review, how many more sessions do you think are required to reach your goals?').

Reviewing progress on a regular basis can provide reinforcement for your client's efforts to effect change in his life, but be careful not to structure such reviews as a 'ticking off' or corrective training as the client may engage in SELF-DEPRECIATION and thereby stall his progress.

reward

We are not referring to a reward that clients might give themselves for carrying out homework tasks, but the reward therapy offers: that by developing an effective problem-solving outlook, the external environment is likely to yield better results for clients (e.g. improved relationships, more opportunities). Whether such rewards are realized over the longer-term can be monitored through follow-up appointments (without them, you will not see if your share of the hard work of therapy has borne fruit). If rewards from the external environment do not appear to be forthcoming or are slower coming than clients anticipated, help them to see that they can regard their own change efforts as the reward (e.g. 'Though I'm still without a partner at the present time, learning to enjoy my own company has made living alone a far more pleasant experience than it used to be').

risk-taking

Personal growth is stunted if risks are not taken. A risk-averse outlook usually means the person accumulates a lifetime of 'if only . . .' regrets (e.g. 'If only I had taken the job when it was offered to me, but I wasn't completely sure I could handle the responsibility'). Not being 'completely sure' is often the reason why people avoid taking risks: there is the possibility that they might experience, for example, failure or rejection which they would evaluate as 'intolerable' or 'awful' (see AWFULIZING). In avoiding the risks associated with developing a more interesting and exciting life, people run the risk of settling for a life of dull and dispiriting predictability.

Risk-taking is not one-sided (i.e. that the feared outcome will occur) but also allows for the possibility of having one's desires fulfilled. Even if the outcome is unfavourable, it is not fixed in perpetuity (e.g. a lifelong failure; forever crushed by rejection) but subject to a continuous process of change, adaptation and learning (e.g. eventually bouncing back from rejection and trying again). Also, judging an unfavourable outcome in relative, not absolute, terms helps to maintain a realistic perspective on setbacks (e.g. 'I did not give a good speech which is unfortunate, but not awful'). While risks need to be carefully considered, not recklessly engaged in, they nevertheless provide a reminder of the difference between merely existing and really living.

S

safety-seeking behaviour

From the client's viewpoint, safety-seeking behaviour prevents a feared catastrophe from occurring (e.g. holding on to something to prevent fainting during a panic attack or saying little in social situations to avoid being revealed as 'stupid'). Do safety-seeking behaviours actually keep clients safe? Only in the short term, whereas in the longer term they prevent disconfirmation of clients' catastrophic cognitions, help to maintain anxiety and, in some cases, increase symptoms, e.g. attempts to suppress intrusive thoughts in obsessive-compulsive disorder actually increase the occurrence of these thoughts (Salkovskis 1996).

The operation of safety behaviours keeps clients feeling unsafe and stuck in fearful anticipation of catastrophe: imminent in panic or distant in health anxiety. Dropping safety behaviours, whether overt or covert, in order to face their fears, helps clients to feel genuinely safe as they are now able to develop non-catastrophic explanations of their symptoms or situations (e.g. saying more and initiating conversation in social situations reveals to the client that others do not see her as stupid which, in turn, encourages her to re-evaluate her self-image). Clients will only drop their safety-seeking behaviours when they understand and accept the rationale for doing so *and* are prepared to tolerate the short-term DISCOMFORT of so doing.

scepticism

Some clients might too readily believe what they tell themselves (e.g. 'I'll always see myself as inadequate') or are told by others (e.g. 'Even my best friend says I'm thick, so it must be true'). In other words, these clients do not question their own or others' ideas. Developing a more sceptical attitude means a corresponding increase in critical thinking and OPEN-MINDEDNESS; it does not mean becoming emotionless, cynical or paralysed by constant self-doubt. On the contrary, we believe that scepticism promotes passion and courage:

> To think for yourself, to start from the position that any statement or belief may, or may not, be true, whatever other people say, and to examine it for yourself, is an act of courage. Be daring in this enterprise.
>
> (Hauck 1988: 11)

In the above example, the client can start adopting a sceptical attitude by asking himself how he knows he will never change his self-image and if LABELLING himself as inadequate is the best way to bring about change in his life. Ellis (1983) suggests that scepticism is one criterion of mental health.

scientific thinking

This involves 'collecting data (problems, thoughts, attitudes), formulating hypotheses, setting up experiments and evaluating results' (Blackburn and Davidson 1995: 51). Some clients might see scientific thinking as an unnatural, ponderous or time-consuming method for reaching valid conclusions about events (e.g. 'I think about things and then get on with it. I don't hang about studying my navel'). With this example, you can ask the client if she would *carefully* consider 'things' she had to think about before making a very important decision in her life or would she rush to judgement in order to avoid navel-gazing? The point to make is that she needs to examine the evidence for her current disturbance-inducing thinking (e.g. 'I can't cope with the pressure at work. I'm weak and pathetic') in order to arrive at more balanced and self-helping conclusions (e.g. 'I am struggling to cope at work, so I might need to ask for more support. Labelling myself because of my problems is neither accurate nor helpful'). Also, navel-gazing is not scientific thinking: the former is profitless introspection while the latter actively seeks finding better ways of solving problems.

self

Clients often have a simple view of the self such as you are what you do (e.g. 'I couldn't answer the question, so this proves I'm stupid'). This view of the self as rateable usually leads to emotional trouble for clients when they are going through difficult times (see RATING). A complex view of the self would see it as unrateable. Hauck defines the self as 'every conceivable thing about you that can be rated' (1991b: 33). 'Every conceivable thing' starts from the moment of one's birth to the moment of one's death. From this viewpoint, it is futile and meaningless to rate the complexity of the self on an aspect of it (e.g. 'So would you say that your fifty years of living and experience can be completely captured by the judgement "I'm stupid"?').

Would clients knowingly teach a simple view of the self to their children (e.g. 'You failed your exams, so you're a failure. Now go to your room. I can't bear to look at a failure')? In our experience, the usual reply is an emphatic 'No'. Learning about the unrateable and complex self often involves a PARADIGM SHIFT. The effort involved in embracing this new concept is usually rewarded by greater emotional stability, both generally and during tough times.

self-acceptance

Self-acceptance means refraining from RATING oneself, but rating only aspects of oneself. Self-acceptance does not involve a loss of IDENTITY because the person has not based it on certain criteria being met (e.g. having a job, friends, success). Loss of identity is more likely to occur with SELF-ESTEEM. If self-acceptance does have any identity it is acknowledging oneself as an unrateable, complex and fallible (imperfect) human being – this view of the self remains constant despite changing circumstances in one's life. This identity can seem as dull as ditchwater when compared to the excitement of being a 'high achiever' and a 'can-do guy'.

However, if the person becomes a 'low achiever' and a 'can't-do guy' another and unwanted identity is likely to be installed (e.g. 'I'm useless and a failure'). Self-acceptance would certainly acknowledge that achievement and success are important aspects of the self but not the whole story of the self. Avoiding pointless self-denigration, learning from current setbacks and striving for success again are based on a new outlook: 'I still want to be a can-do guy, but what I won't do any more is base my identity on it or anything else.'

self-awareness

When a client first comes to therapy his attention is usually externally focused on others or events who have 'caused' his emotional problems – he is often only aware of what he is looking at and unaware of what he is thinking about. Clients can learn to detect their thoughts associated with negative affect by asking what Beck calls the 'cardinal question of cognitive therapy: What was just going through my mind?' (1995: 10). Learning to 'catch' surface cognitions or automatic negative thoughts

(ANTS) allows the client to correct distortions in his thinking (e.g. ALWAYS AND NEVER THINKING and JUMPING TO CONCLUSIONS). Working at the ANTS or symptom level is usually seen as bottom-up processing, i.e. 'Stimulus-driven processing which is triggered by seeing something in the external world which triggers a set of internal cognitive processes' (Butler and McManus 1998: 135).

What makes a client vulnerable to experiencing episodes of emotional disturbance lies deep in his internal world and he needs to be helped by you 'to roll an inner eye around an inner landscape' (to borrow a phrase from the American playwright, Clifford Odets) to locate his core maladaptive beliefs about himself, others and the world. Working at this level is known as top-down processing (i.e. schema-driven). By tapping his internal communications (Beck 1976), the client begins to understand why he feels and behaves the way that he does in certain situations, and what steps will be required of him to initiate and sustain the change process.

self-deception

Clients rarely, if ever, say their problem is self-deception though it may play a role in perpetuating their problems. The issue of self-deception can seem very strange indeed: the client must surely know the truth in order to deceive herself about it otherwise what is she deceiving herself about? How can she lie and not know she is lying? However, for the purposes of this entry, self-deception involves the client listening to the self-talk that she wishes to be true and not paying attention to unpalatable information or facts. (Self-deception can be seen as an extreme form of WISHFUL THINKING – Warburton 2000.) For example, a client refuses to consider the mounting evidence that her husband is possibly having an affair and, instead, insists that 'he would never betray me. Our love is sacred.'

In addressing self-deception, you can encourage the client, as in the above example, to assume as true what she does not want to focus on, i.e. her husband's possible unfaithfulness. What would it mean to her if it was true? The client might reply that her life would be destroyed and she could never again trust or love a man. If she could see her life as battered, but not destroyed, and imagine herself finding love again, would she then be prepared to expend some effort in establishing the facts of her husband's behaviour and asking some tough questions of him? Tackling self-deception is not meant to rub a client's nose in unsavoury facts, but to provide constructive ways of coping with an outcome the client wants to avoid thinking about (see POSITIVE THINKING).

self-depreciation

Self-depreciation occurs when SELF-ESTEEM (i.e. self-value) falls. One definition of depreciate is 'diminish in value'. The self can be seen as stock which other people invest in with love, approval, praise, rewards, etc. and/or the person invests in because she has achieved important goals or lived up to her ideals. At this point, the person's stock is riding high. However, when others or the person disinvests from this stock because of, respectively, disapproval or goal failure, her stock falls or even crashes. Whenever self-value is involved, self-depreciation is not far behind. For the self to be stable, whatever the state of the internal or external 'market', we would recommend the person invests in developing SELF-ACCEPTANCE.

self-disclosure

The first things to say about therapist self-disclosure are: to use it judiciously, not incontinently; determine if your clients value your disclosure (not all will); and to use a coping model of disclosure, not a mastery one. Self-disclosure can be helpful because:

- It offers hope (e.g. 'I had a similar problem which I eventually overcame'), provides a solidarity of suffering, and gives a realistic perspective of change, i.e. it involves personal struggle, not passivity or the avoidance of discomfort.
- It demonstrates that you practise what you preach. You are not a textbook-spouting therapist.
- Your disclosure can encourage reluctant clients to 'open up'.
- It shows you are not a paragon, but a fallible human being who does not expect to have all the answers to clients' problems.
- It normalizes what clients believe are their 'strange' or 'unique' problems.

However, as noted at the outset, some clients are turned off by therapist self-disclosure, so be discriminating in its use and, if you do use it, elicit client feedback about its impact and value.

self-efficacy (Bandura 1977)

Clients' expectations of personal effectiveness and therapeutic outcome usually involve the questions: 'Am I able to do it?' (i.e. carry out the treatment programme) and 'Will what I do lead to the desired outcome?' (i.e. achieve the client's goal). Increasing self-efficacy leads to more independence. Regular self-efficacy appraisals are important to boost clients' confidence and correct any misattributions for their performance accomplishments (e.g. due to you, others, luck or chance). Increasing self-efficacy provides the answer to the question posed by the song, 'Who can I turn to if you turn away?': 'Myself, of course.'

self-esteem

'Esteem' is derived from the verb 'to estimate' which means to give something or someone a rating, judgement or estimation. The concept of self-esteem suggests that a person can be rated globally. Clients with low self-esteem usually have low self-value (e.g. 'I can't be worth much as no one wants to go out with me'). The problem with self-esteem is described by Fennell: 'People hang self-esteem on a range of different pegs. If the peg on which you have hung your sense of worth is taken away, this exposes you to the full force of negative beliefs about yourself' (1999: 207).

Loss of self-esteem can also lead to a loss of identity (e.g. 'Who am I now that my wife has left me?'). The danger with talk of 'raising self-esteem' is that the client might seek new pegs to hang it on thereby perpetuating the mistakes of the past – his restored self-esteem remains precariously balanced – and quickly forgetting that whatever goes up, can also come down. Another difficulty with self-esteem is that

> . . . if you focus on your negative aspects . . . then you are less likely to change them because you are sidetracked by giving your 'self' a global negative rating for having these aspects. It is difficult to change anything while you are berating yourself for having these aspects in the first place.
>
> (Dryden 1998: 32)

The antidote to self-esteem is SELF-ACCEPTANCE which means the person never disesteems himself (though he may some of his actions) because he now accepts himself unconditionally. The robustness of self-acceptance counteracts the fragility of self-esteem.

self-help

Effective therapy is based on effective self-therapy. The ultimate aim of CBT is to help clients become their own lifelong self-therapist: 'My job is to help you help yourself. I can't do the work for you and even if I could, you would be no better off as you would now be dependent on me to sort out your present and future problems.' The essence of self-help is clients applying a self-change methodology without your prompting (when therapy is terminated you will not be there to prompt them). Give your clients opportunities to start practising self-help methods in therapy as early as clinically indicated (e.g. taking the lead in setting the agenda). You can reconceptualize your role as a consultant or coach who provides feedback on their performance and problem-solving abilities. Praise clients' efforts at self-change and attribute success to them, which means that you will have to keep your ego under control if you have a problem with minimizing your own contributions to clients' progress.

shame

In shame, the person perceives his public self-presentation as weak, inadequate or flawed in some way. For example, a person feels ashamed because he revealed to his colleagues that he is a 'pathetic wimp' for crying when his boss gave him a dressing down for poor timekeeping. While in this shameful state, he overestimates the extent to which his colleagues will ridicule him or judge him harshly.

The public self or 'how one lives in the mind of another' (Gilbert 1992) is not the whole story of the SELF. The self is made up of countless aspects and, therefore, for the person to conclude that he is a 'pathetic wimp' on the basis of a particular aspect (crying) indicates OVERGENERAL-IZING and the PART–WHOLE ERROR in his thinking. If the person is able to feel disappointed about but not ashamed of his behaviour, then he can stand back and view it in the compassionate context of self-acceptance, i.e. that his behaviour was an unfortunate response rather than a weakness (Dryden 1997).

Within this compassionate context, he is more likely to make realistic judgements about the reactions of his colleagues to his behaviour – there will be a range of them rather than a sole reaction. Even if some of his colleagues do judge him harshly for crying, the person can decide that how he wants to live in his own mind (with compassion) is more important to him than how he lives in theirs (trying to prove his worth or manliness to them).

shoulds

What should you do when a client says 'should' (e.g. 'I should be more time-efficient')? Our advice is to think carefully and act cautiously as you may not be in the presence of a disturbance-producing should. You will need to find out if the client feels excessively upset about being time-inefficient, engages in prolonged SELF-DEPRECIATION when she is or views the should statement as a rigid rule of living (e.g. 'I absolutely should be more time-efficient').

The meaning of the 'should' should be elicited while keeping in mind that shoulds have several non-dogmatic meanings (see Neenan and Dryden 1999 for a discussion of these meanings). If you twitch and jerk with a triumphant 'Aha!' every time the client says 'should', she may avoid using the word in order to keep you calm! However, this avoidance may keep intact 'should' statements that really do require your clinical attention (e.g. 'I absolutely shouldn't have made that mistake and I'll never forgive myself for it').

skills

If your client does not make use of CBT in her own life after formal therapy has ended, then she will tend not to sustain any changes she has made in therapy. The essence of SELF-HELP in CBT is the deliberate use of CBT skills in the client's own life. It follows from this that a major part of your job as a CBT therapist is to help your client acquire such skills. Skills-based approaches to CBT can be found in Greenberger and Padesky (1995) and Dryden (2001).

As your client progresses in therapy, consider to what extent she is making progress by using appropriate CBT skills and, conversely, when she fails to make progress. If the latter is the case, help your client to identify and overcome obstacles to skills utilization, and to realize that becoming skills-proficient takes repeated practice of these skills, not make or break, one-off attempts to master them. There are many parallels to skills acquisition that you can refer to for clients who struggle to see the value of learning and acquiring CBT skills (e.g. learning to drive, swim, use computers, etc.). Learning new skills provides more opportunities for self-development, freedom and enjoyment; acquiring CBT skills helps clients to remove the emotional and behavioural blocks to these opportunities.

social interest

A term used by Adler (1964) to take into account the concerns and interests of the wider community when a client is planning her goals. Within this framework, the client's goals will be balanced: pro-self and pro-social. We would describe this framework as enlightened social interest (see ENLIGHTENED SELF-INTEREST). Some clients might object to considering the wider community's concerns during goal negotiation (e.g. 'I'm the one with the problem, not them!'). You can point out that their chosen goals could harm others, appear selfish or are ethically irresponsible and therefore could rebound upon them (e.g. becoming socially isolated again or not being trusted). As Walen et al. observe:

> Most of us have as one of our goals of happiness to relate to many people
> compatibly and to a few people intimately . . . It is not in our best interests to
> act unfairly, inconsiderately, or selfishly.
>
> (Walen et al. 1992: 10)

'society is to blame'

Society routinely gets the blame for a multitude of problems, so when a
client points an accusatory finger at society, a critical analysis is called
for. Who (name names) or what (e.g. institutions, agencies) are the
'guilty ones'? For example, a client I (MN) saw said that 'society makes
you feel worthless without a job' (he recently lost his). First of all, losing
his job (objective fact) and believing he is worthless without one
(subjective evaluation) are two separate issues – had he connected them
or had society?

We examined how he was 'treated by society'. The dismissal letter
from his employer did not contain any defamatory comments; his family,
relatives and friends were supportive; he could not think of a single
comment from any of the main political parties, the media or the
Church that denigrated the unemployed. He said that going to 'sign on'
was humiliating, but reluctantly agreed that none of the staff he spoke
to at the benefits agency treated him as undeserving or suggested he
was a malingerer. The evidence he eventually accumulated that 'society
was to blame' was a tabloid press article on the 'work-shy' and some
unsympathetic comments from a man he spoke to in a pub ('Anybody
can get a job if they want to. There's no excuse for being unemployed.
It's just sheer idleness'). Why was he focused on this article and the
'saloon bar bore' rather than on all the other viewpoints on offer?

The bottom line was that *he* equated being unemployed with being
worthless. He said that his father 'had always drummed into me that
being out of work was a mark of shame'. Since he lost his job, he carried
this SHAME with him everywhere: if he could see that he was worthless,
then so could everyone else (that is why he found going to 'sign on' so
humiliating). Even though he had absorbed this powerful message from
his father, he had not sought to moderate it in his own mind over the
years (he said he certainly would not teach this message to his children).

The client was able to see eventually that he was responsible for his
beliefs, not society, and that continuing to think in this way hampered
his efforts to find another job and undermined his self-confidence.
Even if the client had received a lot of unkind comments from others
about being unemployed, he still had the ability to make up his own
mind about this issue and learn to think more critically about the
messages from others. If society was indeed to blame for his problems,

then who or what else would be needed in therapy to sort them out for him?

Like Gilbert, we are not advancing the view 'that we are in some sense socially decontextualized beings who disturb ourselves only by our thoughts' (2000: 202). If a client does believe he is being maligned, marginalized or unfairly targeted in some way, he can always pursue social justice by, among other things, joining a pressure group, lobbying his MP and local councillor, or writing letters to newspapers. However, before he does that, he wants to be crystal clear in his own mind that he is not maligning, depreciating or marginalizing himself in any way. Therefore, when he puts the blame on society for his emotional problems, it is frequently because he himself believes the message that he thinks 'society' is purveying.

specificity

Your clinical conversation with a client should be based on specificity such as asking her to provide specific examples of her general problem. In order to encourage specificity, remind her that a specific example occurs at a specific time in a specific place and with specific people present (if relevant). By making the example as concrete as possible, the client could make a video recording of it (Neenan and Dryden 2001). Imagine trying to make a video recording of a general problem.

When a concrete example has been provided, ask the client to pinpoint her specific thoughts, feelings and behaviours in this situation. Modelling specificity for your client means clear, direct and concise communication. Allowing her or yourself to ramble or talk in vague terms means that therapy will be unfocused thereby producing a poor outcome for the client.

standard arguments

Standard arguments based on 'Where's the evidence for that belief?' and 'Is it logical to conclude that about yourself?' can be productive for some clients in helping them to restructure their maladaptive thinking. For other clients, these arguments have little, if any, impact on their thinking (e.g. 'I couldn't care less about evidence or logic'). The standard textbook arguments are not engendering any new viewpoints for these clients.

To arouse their interest, you need to arouse your own – you will not be creative by following a textbook formula. Therefore, be on the alert for good ideas or arguments from books, plays, films, essays, articles, television, overheard conversations; in other words, from any source.

Have a regular 'arguments group' with colleagues where you discuss and develop good ideas to add to your repertoire. Hauck states that when you

> . . . have made an extremely relevant comment to your client you will often recognize that you have touched a deep nerve by the way the client listens. Look at the eyes. They are intensely focused on you. There is no evidence of boredom or of self-consciousness . . . It is a moment like this which Rudolf Dreikurs, the Adlerian, called the 'recognition reflex'.
>
> (Dreikurs 1968; Hauck 1980a: 117)

I (MN) saw a client who was prone to hitting others when he was called unpleasant names or felt he was being ridiculed in some way. He said this was the strong and manly thing to do even though he was in constant trouble with the police for his violent behaviour. My standard arguments fell on deaf ears until he told me of his interest in Westerns (a mutual interest). I steered the conversation to the scene in *The Magnificent Seven* where the Charles Bronson character talks about the real nature of courage and being a man (learning to endure the vicissitudes of life rather than following a life of violence as a gunfighter). He liked and acted on the idea that enduring the insults of others was real strength. Lashing out, he concluded, was a sign of a weak mind because that shows others control you with their insults.

suggestibility

This 'is a vulnerability to the influential ideas of others' (Feltham and Dryden 1993: 185). For example, a client, who placed too much faith in his friend's advice, was angry when he lost a lot of money betting on a horse that his friend said was a 'sure thing'. Suggestibility is not thinking things through for oneself or questioning the views of others – in other words, a form of MENTAL LAZINESS. Suggest to your client that he develops a third-person perspective that enables him to 'eavesdrop' on a conversation between himself and another. With the advice he gets from the other person, would he encourage his partner, children or best friend to act on it? If he replies, 'No, I wouldn't', you can then ask what stops him following his own advice. To combat suggestibility, clients can learn to chew over the advice of others with the words, 'Let me think about it.'

tasks

'Cognitive-behavioural therapy is not a passive experience for patients. It requires your active involvement to work . . . and to do self-help homework that you and your therapist plan and assign' (Leahy and Holland 2000: 88). Clients have tasks to execute both within and without sessions in order to achieve their goals, so they need to develop an action-oriented outlook (see TRYING VS. DOING). Tasks are so important because clients may gain an understanding of the factors that maintain their problems (insight), but it is acting on this insight that achieves a modification or removal of these maintaining factors (e.g. a client sees that his need for approval maintains his dependency on others, so he starts to 'speak his mind' as a first step towards becoming more independent). We might say that what you see and what you do equals therapeutic change, whereas what you see but do not do leaves you with very little apart from the consolation of insight.

termination

You might have OVERVALUED IDEAS about termination (e.g. clients always feel sad about the end of therapy), maybe stemming from believing too readily the psychodynamic view of termination which is that clients inevitably see it as a major loss in their life. To find out what termination really means to your clients, ask them! Refrain from MIND-READING or assuming that your feelings accurately reflect clients' feelings (e.g. the client might be business-like about termination while you become a little tearful). If breaking the relationship does become a major issue for the client then she

> . . . is not ready to terminate, for this is an indication that the client relies on the therapist to fulfill some perceived need – perhaps approval, reassurance, or freedom from responsibility.
>
> (Wessler and Wessler 1980: 182)

If you view termination with grim finality, i.e. you will never see the client again, remember your relationship with your GP. When you say 'Thank you and goodbye' to him, presumably you believe you might need his services again. Some terminations of therapy are temporary ones as these clients will 'call back' at a later date.

themes

Key themes can be discerned in emotional disorders: for example, threat or danger in anxiety; loss and failure in depression; moral lapse or violation in guilt; public disclosure of weakness in shame; and betrayal and unfairness in hurt. Alerting clients to these themes helps them to pinpoint their situation-specific thoughts:

Client: I'm anxious when my wife's brother visits but I'm not sure why.

Therapist: The theme in anxiety is of a threat. Now in what way does his visit pose a threat to you?

Client: (musing) Well, he's always bragging about how much money he earns – he works as a stockbroker – and . . . (voice trails away).

Therapist: And if he does all that bragging . . . ?

Client: I suppose I reflect on my own success or lack of it.

Therapist: What do you mean by 'lack of it'?

Client: Well, compared to him, I'm a failure. When he's gone I do feel low for a while, brooding on what I've done, or rather, what I haven't done with my life.

(The client's feelings change from anxiety to depression after his brother-in-law has departed – his thoughts now reflect the themes in depression.)

Therapist: So would you say that the threat posed by his visit is to your self-esteem or self-value? In other words, does his success remind you of your lack of success for which you will evaluate yourself as a failure?

Client: Yes I would. Now the threat is clear.

Cleaning the 'pane of specificity' (i.e. an analysis of a specific situation) allows the client to look through the window on his life, so to speak, and see whether the theme of failure is present in other areas of his life (e.g. mixing with people who have university degrees – 'They will make me feel inferior'; or who exude confidence – 'They will just remind me how unconfident and weak I really am').

therapeutic relationship

The therapeutic relationship in CBT is regarded as conducive to therapeutic change but insufficient to produce it. The therapeutic relationship is like the soil in which plants can grow. We need the soil of empathy, warmth and genuineness to prepare the ground of change, but without the seeds of change (i.e. techniques) and frequent watering (i.e. client effort to implement the techniques), the plant (i.e. the client) will not fully blossom!

thinking

We all think, but not always in constructive and problem-solving ways. One of your key roles in therapy is to help clients think more critically about their own thinking in relation to their problems. The term 'critically' does not mean endless fault-finding but the ability to analyse problems, see events from different perspectives, weigh evidence, draw conclusions from it unaffected by bias. To put it more simply, learning to think straight instead of crookedly.

Learning to think straight starts with teaching clients that their thoughts are not necessarily accurate – accuracy is reached through REASON and REALITY-TESTING. For example, a client who claims to be hopeless at *everything* can be asked how he managed to get dressed, eat breakfast, catch a bus, get to the session on time, answer your questions, etc. If the client replies he did not mean hopeless at everything, then what specifically is he hopeless at? (already the client is being taught to be more focused and clear in his thinking about the extent of his problem).

Specific examples of the client's perceived hopelessness can be examined to determine his definition of hopelessness, e.g. 'Not being able to master tasks immediately'. What prevents the client from seeing, based on the evidence, that this is an unattainable level of competence and, continually striving to achieve it, perpetuates his problems? Subjecting clients' ideas to critical examination helps them to break out of their closed system of thinking and consider other viewpoints that are likely to be more helpful in solving their problems. Thinking critically is essential 'if the imagination is to be stirred, if the intellect is to work, if mental life is not to sink to a low ebb, and the pursuit of truth (or justice, or self-fulfilment) is not to cease' (Berlin, quoted in Magee 1982: 3).

thoughts and feelings

Inserting the word 'feel' into a statement does not turn the statement into a feeling such as 'I feel that my best friend is upset with me'. The client is expressing a thought, not a feeling; to elicit a feeling you can ask: 'How do you feel about this idea that your best friend is upset with you?' The client might reply: 'I feel that he is going to keep his distance from me.' Again, another thought. Greenberger and Padesky suggest that 'as a general rule, moods can be identified in one descriptive word [e.g. shame, guilt, anxiety, hurt]. If it takes you more than one word to describe a mood, you may be describing a thought' (1995: 28). With this rule in mind, the client says he feels 'anxious' because he thinks, 'I might lose his friendship and I wouldn't be able to cope with that.'

Teaching clients the difference between thoughts and feelings is important because (a) how we feel is based on how we think – therefore, in order to change how we feel, we first have to change how we think; and (b) changing emotion directly is difficult (it usually lags behind changes in thoughts and behaviour), so it is easier to do it indirectly through changing thinking. If you challenge clients' 'I feel . . .' statements without explaining this difference, they might believe you are attacking their 'feelings'. Genuine feelings, not thoughts masquerading as feelings, are not open to dispute:

> . . . they are phenomenological experiences for which only the individual has data. You cannot argue with such subjective states, whereas thoughts, beliefs, and opinions are open to challenge.
>
> (Walen et al. 1992: 98)

Some clients might believe that CBT focuses on thoughts to the exclusion of affect. However, this is incorrect as disturbed feelings need to be pinpointed in order to uncover and modify associated 'hot' (i.e. emotionally charged) thoughts. As Blackburn and Davidson state: 'Cognitive therapy *cannot* take place without first eliciting relevant emotional reactions' (1995: 203; original authors' emphasis).

The close interaction of thoughts and feelings can be seen in Beck calling emotions 'the royal road to cognition' and cognitions 'the royal road to emotion' (quoted in Padesky 1993b: 404). For example, activating a client's guilt in the session reveals these 'hot' thoughts: 'I shouldn't have smacked my child so hard. I should have been able to control her without hitting her. I'm a terrible mother for hurting her.' If the client produced the thoughts in the absence of stating how she felt, listening to the THEMES running through her thoughts would have revealed that she felt guilty (theme: moral lapse or violation).

time-limited irrationalities (Dryden 1994a)

These are disturbance-producing ideas of relatively short duration because the person is able to stand back and think more rationally about the situation (e.g. flying into a rage for several minutes because the person cannot find her car keys, 'They should be by the fucking telephone where I left them!', then calming down and trying to pinpoint where they might actually be). It is unlikely that people consider their time-limited irrationalities to be problems that need addressing in therapy. If you attempt to tackle your clients' time-limited irrationalities, you might suggest to them that they are not allowed to be fallible at all and such irrationalities inevitably point to an underlying pathology. Exceptions to this observation would be, for example, with a client who has a history of aggression and whose next angry outburst might seriously injure or even kill someone. With this client, helping him to limit further, or even extinguish, his time-limited outbursts would be the goal of therapy.

We would suggest that you focus on clients' irrational ideas that are time-prolonging, problem-perpetuating and seem difficult or impossible to dislodge (e.g. a client's long-standing belief, 'I'm not good enough', keeps him miserable, lonely and fearful of intimate involvement).

time management

Time flies; but is the person the passenger or pilot? Being the pilot means the person knows what she wants to achieve in her life while being the passenger may indicate a tendency to drift or an uncertainty of purpose. Effective time management is effective self-management. Self-management starts with clarifying a person's goals and values and then keeping a daily time-log for a week or two to discover how she actually spends her time – does her use of time support her values and take her closer to her goals?

Blocks to effective time management revealed by the use of time-logs include:

- trying to put a QUART INTO A PINT POT
- saying 'Yes' to every request
- believing that one's own interests should never come first
- striving to always do a perfect job when a competent one would be sufficient in the circumstances
- procrastinating over starting tasks or completing paperwork
- letting meetings or interviews consistently overrun.

If effective time management is to be an enduring reality rather than a passing fad, the person needs to keep asking herself, 'What is really important?' As Jones remarks: 'By asking yourself this question every day, you can ensure that both your actions and goals are in alignment' (1998: 93). For example, if a person's work-based goal is to ensure that meetings finish on time, then it is necessary for her, as the chairperson, to interrupt tactfully verbose and rambling colleagues and remind them to be concise and stick to the agenda. Achieving this goal is now more important to her than seeking her colleagues' approval which previously inhibited such interruptions.

transference

This refers to a client reacting to the therapist as he does to significant others in his life. Beck et al. suggest that the therapist 'should allow negative reactions to him or her to arise . . . [as] these reactions to the therapist open windows into the patient's private world' (1990: 65). Transference reactions are treated in the same way as other maladaptive thoughts and beliefs: identified, examined, reality-tested and modified. In this way, clients can learn to step back from their transference reactions and observe what is going on, i.e. repeating self-defeating patterns of behaviour in therapy. For example, a client might show signs of frustration every time he is asked by the therapist, 'What do you think?' This frustration is based on him having to think for himself rather than automatically deferring to authority figures in his life – 'I expect them to tell me what to do.' The client believes that if he has to think for himself it will end in disaster. Experiments can be devised to test the accuracy of his predictions (e.g. taking his partner to a restaurant of his choosing), increase his experience of SELF-EFFICACY and combat his MENTAL LAZINESS (see COUNTERTRANSFERENCE).

trial and error

Problem-solving usually involves trial and error. When clients ask, 'Will it work?', you can reply, 'Let's see' (learning occurs *whatever* the outcome). Each error revealed by each trial can be analysed to inform the next attempt at problem-solving. However, some clients will want an immediately successful trial and no error. You can point out that such an expectation goes against the grain of human progress over the last two millennia (e.g. we take the light bulb for granted but forget the tireless efforts of Thomas Edison to produce it; he famously remarked that 'Genius is one per cent inspiration, ninety-nine per cent perspiration'). How does the client propose to bypass this form of learning with regard to his own progress?

Developing HIGH FRUSTRATION TOLERANCE helps the client to persist (and perspire) with the process of trial and error to achieve a successful outcome, e.g. 'The trials are necessary to reveal the errors which I can then correct in order to achieve my goal, so I'm not going to give up.'

troubleshooting

This means you are on the look-out for obstacles to client change and seek collaborative ways of removing these obstacles when they occur. For example, troubleshooting during homework negotiation (e.g. 'Is there anything that might prevent you from carrying out the task?') might reveal that the client believes he is likely forget to do the homework or he has not got the time to do it. Discussing there and then how he can make it likely that he will remember to carry out the task (e.g. leave a Post-it note on the bathroom mirror) or find the time to do it (e.g. getting up earlier in the morning) helps the client to become his own troubleshooter as part of his developing role as a self-therapist. You can liken your own role as a troubleshooter to being a 'cognitive cop', i.e. apprehending and dealing with clients' thoughts and beliefs that interfere with their progress.

trying vs. doing

Some clients might say 'I'll try' when you ask them if they will carry out their between-session tasks (we are assuming that these tasks have been negotiated, clients see the sense in doing them and have the skills to carry them out). 'Trying' suggests that some effort will be made but lacks the commitment that 'doing' denotes, i.e. persistent and forceful action to achieve a goal. Some clients may have been trying for years to overcome a particular problem but with little success. Do they still want to hold onto this unproductive attitude in therapy?

Even when clients stress that they will 'try harder', they often just do more of the same behaviour that prevents task completion. For example, a client forcefully tells herself to speak up in a group and says at the next homework review, 'I gave myself a really hard time over it', but did not actually speak up – the doing is still absent! Only when the doing starts, can she evaluate the results and see if her catastrophic predictions of being laughed at are realized. Another way of viewing trying is seeing it as an urge associated with, but not necessarily leading to, doing, i.e. an internal mobilization preparing the client for action without actually engaging in it. An urge is a precursor to action, not the action itself.

To emphasize this distinction between doing and trying, ask clients to try to leave the room at the end of the session without doing so or try to drive home without actually driving off – with trying, they cannot be sure of success. To reinforce this point, ask clients to consider their reaction if their children said 'I'll try' with regard to doing their school homework or tidying up their bedroom. A usual reply is that they would be suspicious because they know what trying really means and, therefore, they would tell their children: 'Don't try, do it!'

tyranny

See MUSTS.

uncertainty

Intolerance of uncertainty stems from the demand 'I must know now!' What the person 'must know now!' is (a) what the outcome will be, whether good or bad, or (b) that his fears will not be realized. Since the person cannot know the outcome before it has occurred, his preoccupation with an unknowable outcome acts as a form of water torture, i.e. his anxiogenic thoughts are incessant drips of water in his mind, e.g. 'What will happen? How much longer do I have to wait? Why can't they tell me now? Surely it doesn't have to take this long for an answer? What if I can't cope with bad news?' This intolerance of uncertainty can be linked to a range of situations in the person's life. For example, when he asks a woman out, he insists that she has to give him an answer then and there, he procrastinates over starting a project because he cannot be assured of success, and, whenever possible, buys the same clothes to avoid worrying if new designs and styles 'will look right on me'.

Accepting uncertainty, without having to like it, starts with the person acknowledging that we live in a world of probability and chance where absolute certainties do not and probably will never exist. If the person cannot get an immediate answer to calm his worries, he can focus on the knowable certainties in his life (i.e. his daily routine), divert his energies into more pleasurable activities and plan a range of coping responses to deal with the outcome, whatever it is, instead of AWFULIZING about it. Tolerating uncertainty can teach the person new skills (e.g. 'I can learn to wait without disturbing myself about it') and thereby help him to see that uncertainty can bring some unexpected good as well as the potentially bad.

understanding vs. integration

Understanding involves a client seeing how a rational or self-helping outlook will have beneficial effects upon her maladaptive thoughts, distressing feelings and counterproductive behaviours. Understanding is associated with a weak conviction or belief in this new rational outlook. Integration involves both understanding and action, i.e. the client sees the benefits of a rational outlook and practises this new outlook on a daily or frequent basis in order to internalize it. Integration is associated with a strong conviction or belief in her rational outlook. From the client's viewpoint, understanding is located in the head while integration is experienced in the gut (see INSIGHT).

You can make an analogy with self-assembly furniture: a person can read the instructions and know what needs to be done in order to assemble a table, but unless she starts and persists with assembling it, her new table will remain an object of desire in her head instead of occupying a corner of her living room.

user manual

If you have bought an electrical appliance recently, you will know that it probably came with a user manual. These are the instructions about the appliance that the user needs to follow in order to get the best out of the appliance.

When working with clients who disturb themselves about others' behaviour (because these others are not behaving as they should do or behaving as they should not do), it is useful to ask such clients to imagine that these other people come with a user manual. The task then becomes getting to know the other person and how he or she 'ticks', so clients can get the best out of their contact with them. You can then help your clients to understand that demanding the other person should be different from what he or she actually is will not change that person, since he or she is operating according to their own user manual, not the idealized but inaccurate manual that the client has in mind for the other person.

vagueness

CBT requires SPECIFICITY in trying to understand clients' problems. For example, if a client says his problem is 'around' or 'about' relationships, he is not telling you very much and if this vagueness continues, therapy will remain marooned at the level of vague generalities. What, specifically, is the problem with relationships?

Client: It's the intimacy thing.
Therapist: Do you mean getting close to someone?
Client: Yes, the closeness bit.
Therapist: What might happen if you get close to someone?
Client: Well, you know . . .
Therapist: Actually, I don't know. That's what I want to find out.
Client: Well, you show someone your feelings and then . . .
Therapist: And then . . . what?
Client: Well, you open up to someone, then they ridicule you or reject you, something like that.
Therapist: So would you say that the key problem for you with relationships is this: if you get close to someone you believe they will ridicule or reject you? Is that right? (client nods).

Vagueness prevents understanding: if the client does not know precisely what the problem is, how can he formulate an effective response to it? Also, vagueness can provide a 'protective belt' around the client, i.e. he does not have to commit himself to a particular course of action. Make therapy a 'vagueness-free zone' by emphasizing to your clients that clear and precise information is required.

values

When a client feels angry, depressed, ashamed or guilty about not acting in accordance with her values, it is important to help the client first

147

undisturb herself emotionally about the situation before discussing these values. This discussion focuses on exploring some of her values to determine if they are rigidly adhered to (hence the emotional disturbance when they are not adhered to), have outlived their usefulness or have been unquestioningly accepted from others.

For example, a client felt guilty because, when she looked at her children, she had doubts at times about whether she really wanted to be a mother. Her guilt stemmed from believing: 'I must never have any doubts about whether I want my children. If I have such doubts, this proves I'm a thoroughly bad mother.' Also, she had unquestioningly accepted her mother's viewpoint that children are a 'blessing from God and any real woman should be truly grateful for having them'. When the client's guilt moderated and she was able to think about these issues from a non-disturbed perspective, she said that she did not support her mother's viewpoint (e.g. 'You can be a real woman with or without children') and having doubts about motherhood was compatible with her revised values of what constitutes 'being a good mother'.

verbosity

When we listen to therapists' audiotapes of their sessions with clients, verbosity is usually present, e.g. 'So you're anxious about meeting your new boyfriend's parents. I wonder what's going on there for you? I wonder if it says something about presentation of the self to others. The anxiety itself is a form of communication about what may be going on inside your head.' All the therapist had to ask to start the process of Socratic enquiry was: 'What are you anxious about?' We suggest that you approach the use of words like a miser – carefully! This approach will not only concentrate your mind, but also your client's; if she has to listen to your verbosity, this will distract her from focusing on her own thinking.

Client verbosity, like yours, is a waste of valuable time and adds nothing of clarity, value or efficiency to therapy. To encourage clients to be more concise in their communication with you, ask them what effect it would have on their communication if you charged them per word. Would they prefer the session fee to be based on verbosity or conciseness?

vicious circle

Clients often get caught up in vicious circles of thinking, feeling and behaving maladaptively. For example:

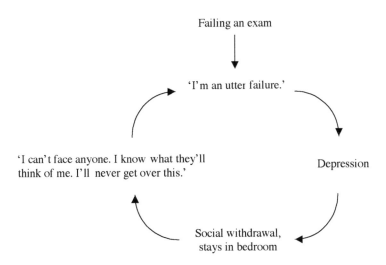

Failing an exam

'I'm an utter failure.'

Depression

'I can't face anyone. I know what they'll
think of me. I'll never get over this.'

Social withdrawal,
stays in bedroom

The client's maladaptive conclusion ('I'm an utter failure') on the basis
of the event (failing an exam) leads to his depression and social
withdrawal which, in turn, protects him from exposing his 'failure' to
others and incurring, in his mind, rejection or disapproval. The client
sees no way out of his present predicament. The client's distorted and
negative way of interpreting events maintains his vicious circle.

Moving from a vicious circle to a virtuous circle (i.e. a beneficial
recurring cycle of cause and effect) involves viewing events in a non-
distorted way and constructing new self-helping beliefs. For example:

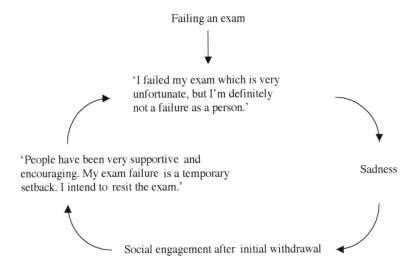

Failing an exam

'I failed my exam which is very
unfortunate, but I'm definitely
not a failure as a person.'

Sadness

'People have been very supportive and
encouraging. My exam failure is a temporary
setback. I intend to resit the exam.'

Social engagement after initial withdrawal

The client no longer links exam failure to self-failure, does not 'hide away' from others, sees that the unpleasant experience of exam failure is time-limited, not eternal, and vows to resit his exams. In this virtuous circle, the client is now thinking, feeling and behaving adaptively and faces the challenges and setbacks in his life instead of withdrawing from them as in the vicious circle.

vulnerability

Show your clients where in their life they are vulnerable to emotional disturbance and how this vulnerability is maintained. For example, when a client spends time on his own, his mood drops and his alcohol consumption and smoking go up. What goes through his mind to affect him in this way? The same thoughts each time: 'I can't entertain myself. I don't like my own company. In fact, I can't stand it. I must have people around me.' This is an extreme way of appraising solitude and thereby perpetuates his inability to cope with it.

However, the client's solution to remove this vulnerability from his life was to find a partner to live with him. Even though more of his time would be filled by his partner, the vulnerability would remain while he still feared his own company (what if she went away for the weekend or dumped him?). Further episodes of emotional disturbance could be reliably predicted unless he found ways of making his own company more tolerable (see LONELINESS).

warning signs

A client is puzzled why she did not pay attention to the 'warning signs' (e.g. aggressiveness, heavy drinking, use of derogatory terms) in the early stages of a relationship that eventually turned out to be abusive and violent. Why she turned a blind eye to these warning signs can involve SELF-DECEPTION, idealization of the person (e.g. 'He's every woman's dream'), fulfilling her own sexual and emotional needs (e.g. 'I am so sick of being alone'), or not wanting to be the 'odd one out' (i.e. partnerless) among her friends.

Whatever the reason(s), it is important for the client to re-enter her frame of mind in the early stages of the relationship to understand her behaviour (e.g. 'When he got drunk and called me a "slag", I put it down to pressure at work. When he hit me, I wondered if it was my fault in some way. I was so desperate for the relationship to work out that I kept on looking for excuses for his behaviour'). Examining and modifying the thoughts and beliefs that led to her ignoring the warning signs can help her to act more promptly if these signs appear again in her next relationship ('One sign and I'm out of there').

'what I learned from you'

Also known by the acronym WILFY (Elliott 1995), this technique focuses on past learning, particularly from childhood. The client identifies a belief or rule from the past (e.g. 'Never depend on anyone'), its source (e.g. her father) and the costs of adhering to it (e.g. compulsive self-reliance at the expense of intimacy and trust in others), tells the person he was wrong about what he taught her (without seeking to be destructive in her criticism), and then formulates a new adaptive rule or belief (e.g. 'I don't want to be so self-reliant. I want to learn that I can depend on some people and show my vulnerabilities to them'). This technique is conducted with the client imagining that the person from the past is sitting in an empty chair while she is talking to him.

We would add that the WILFY method helps the client to see why unhelpful past messages are maintained in the present because she continues to subscribe to them. WILFY enables the client to examine the validity of the message and construct a new (and maybe overdue) self-helping reply to it.

'what if . . . ?' thinking

'What if . . . ?' catastrophic thinking (e.g. 'What if I can't answer the questions? What if my hands start to shake? What if the audience finds me boring?') is a consequence of worry which, in turn, is an intolerance of UNCERTAINTY and doubt (e.g. 'I must know that I will perform competently in running the workshop'). 'What if . . . ?' thinking overestimates the feared catastrophe occurring and underestimates the person's ability to cope constructively with it if it does occur. Engaging in 'what if . . . ?' thinking is hardly likely to prevent an adverse outcome from occurring. As Ellis observes:

> Most *possible* disasters do not actually occur, and millions of minor mistakes hardly lead to disastrous results. Remember the wise statement of Mark Twain, 'My life has been filled with terrible misfortunes – most of which never happened!'
>
> (2001: 97; original author's emphasis)

Some clients believe that 'what if . . . ?' thinking is a form of problem-solving (e.g. 'If you identify all the possible "what ifs . . . ?", then you'll be able to deal with them'). However, what usually happens is that by identifying a series of 'what ifs . . . ?', these clients are just problem-generating in ever more catastrophic fashion without developing a coping plan in response to the 'what ifs . . . ?' Padesky and Greenberger (1995) state that 'what if . . . ?' anxious thinking can be transformed into 'then what . . . ?' problem-solving thinking. For example:

Question: What if I can't answer the question?
Response: Then say you can't. Ask if anyone in the audience can answer it. If no one can, then say you will find out the answer and move on to the next question.
Question: What if my hands start to shake?
Response: Then that shows you're nervous. Nothing wrong with that. If you accept yourself for being nervous, then the shaking will probably subside. If it doesn't, then clasp your hands behind your back for a while.
Question: What if the audience finds me boring?

Response: Then if this is the case, you will need some training in livening
              yourself up before you run another workshop.

Another response to 'what if . . . ?' anxious thinking is to say 'So what if
. . . ?'; this is not a statement of indifference, but one of determination to
deal with the problem (Lazarus et al. 1993). For example, 'So what if I'm
told by my doctor that I have a terminal illness? I may take a couple of
days for this grim news to sink in, then I will plan how to spend my
remaining time as enjoyably as possible.' Newman suggests that a
creative use of 'what if . . .' thinking is to give equal consideration to
positive 'what ifs . . .':

> Clients rarely if ever give equal time to the positive, literally *opposite*
> question, 'What if I succeed?' Therein lies a fundamental cognitive bias,
> because an objective assessment of future outcomes requires the careful
> consideration of both the positive and negative possibilities.
>   (Newman 2000: 140; original author's emphasis)

With the more fundamental question of intolerance of uncertainty and
doubt, the person needs to give up seeking guarantees that bad things
will not happen and, instead, embrace probability vs. possibility
outcomes (e.g. 'I think the workshop will probably work out reasonably
well but, if it doesn't, then the important thing is the feedback from the
audience to learn from, not wailing "woe is me" and seeing it as the end
of everything').

what is going on (WIGO)

This is accepting the world as it actually is rather than demanding how it
should be. Accepting empirical reality does not mean passivity or resignation in the face of it or condoning it if it is negative. By checking facts
against prevailing reality, clients can determine if their beliefs are consis-
tent with reality. For example, a client kept making mistakes at work and
kept insisting, 'I shouldn't be making mistakes'; in other words, reality
should not be reality. In his case, we can ask: what is going on with his
thinking? By adopting the stance of a PERSONAL SCIENTIST, he now
announced, 'I should be making mistakes because that is exactly what
I'm doing.' His view of reality now corresponded with empirical reality.
He was then able to focus on PROBLEM-SOLVING instead of wasting his time
and energy on 'KING CANUTE' THINKING.

'why me?'

See JUST WORLD-VIEW.

will-power

Ellis defines will-power 'not merely as the determination to change but the determination to *work* at changing oneself and the *actual work* that one does to follow up this determination' (1980: 22; original author's italics). Clients can compare their idiosyncratic definitions of will-power with Ellis's as a way of assessing the strength of their COMMITMENT to change. In essence, will-power is doing whatever it takes to get the job done (i.e. achieve the goal). Some clients say they lack will-power to effect change in their life but, paradoxically, show determination not to change through prolonged RESISTANCE and endless 'YES, BUT . . .' THINKING. We call this 'won't-power', a self-defeating form of will-power that maintains the status quo in the client's life instead of changing it. You can undertake with the client a cost-benefit analysis of 'won't-power' vs. will-power.

Other clients may continually emphasize their earnest resolve to change (stressing *will*, the cognitive aspect), but fail to follow through on the *power* (denoting action, the behavioural aspect). Will without power creates little real change (Ellis 2001).

wishful thinking

Wishful thinking is 'extremely common, and very tempting because it allows us to avoid unpalatable truths' (Warburton 2000: 145; see SELF-DECEPTION). Wishing it so, can make it so in the person's mind . . . until frustration intrudes when the wish collides with an unyielding reality (De Botton 2001). For example, a client believes that his excessive drinking does not interfere with his work and his colleagues 'don't notice it anyway', but one morning he is called to his boss's office and told to seek professional help for his drinking or face disciplinary proceedings. If he wants to keep his job, then he can no longer take refuge in wishful thinking.

Not all wishful thinking is harmful or self-defeating: reality-based wishful thinking acknowledges the desire but accepts the truth of the situation, e.g. 'I will deal with the situation as it actually is, even though I wish it were otherwise.'

workaholism

We divide workaholism into two types: compulsive and non-compulsive. Compulsive workaholics are driven by such beliefs as 'I must work and achieve to prove I'm a worthwhile person' or 'I have to keep working as I can't stand idleness because I start constantly worrying'.

Workaholism eventually takes its toll: 'The workaholic behavior pattern is typical of the Type A individual who . . . experiences a much higher risk of heart attack. The workaholic remains chronically in a state of distress' (Quick et al. 1997: 224). The balance in the workaholic's life is excessively or exclusively tilted towards work to the detriment of outside relationships, activities and home life.

The non-compulsive workaholic or workaphile

> . . . does not use work as a defence against anxiety or emotional involvement, but works because he or she actively *enjoys* working and the results that come from it [and] strongly *prefers* effort to idleness or relaxation, but can be quite happy without it, though less happy than when actively engaged in meaningful work.
>
> (Dryden and Gordon 1993b: 123; original authors' italics)

The compulsive workaholic believes he has no choice other than to drive himself relentlessly while the non-compulsive workaphile chooses to make work a major part of his life but also realizes other choices are available to him (e.g. taking a holiday, going to the theatre).

Some workaholics are, paradoxically, procrastinators (e.g. 'What? I'm the busiest person in the department'). Even though they appear to be very busy, the work they produce is actually 'busywork' (Knaus 1998). This means they might be working on many projects but do not meet their deadlines or produce quality work – they are 'paper shufflers'. This occurs because they fail to prioritize their work or take on too much work. They cannot see the wood for the workaholism.

X-factor

Some clients may have great difficulty in talking about a problem (e.g. sexual abuse) because they will experience intense SHAME or GUILT in doing so, e.g. 'I'm afraid to bring it out into the open. I don't believe I can trust anyone with this problem.' Instead of trying to winkle the problem out of the client and perhaps creating even greater client reluctance to reveal it, we suggest calling the problem the 'X-factor' and talking in general terms about how to cope with it:

> The most important thing that a person can do is to accept herself for having the X-factor and stop condemning, attacking or hating herself for having it. Compassion towards herself is much needed to tackle the X-factor. The next step is for the person to see how she lets the X-factor persist in her life through some of the beliefs she holds. For example, if she told others about it, she might fear being rejected, ridiculed or reviled. If she could learn to trust someone, she might find a very different reaction and also hear some helpful viewpoints on tackling her problem. Also, the X-factor is not the whole story of herself or her life, but obviously a painful part of it. Taking the risk of talking about it helps her to feel less overwhelmed by the X-factor and see that there is light at the end of the tunnel.

The client can 'chew over' between sessions whether or not to disclose her problem to you or start working on it herself without your help. The client may not start to address the problem until months after formal therapy has ended and the 'X-factor' approach may then have a sleeper effect on helping her to resolve it.

I (MN) saw a client who said she felt extremely guilty about a past event which involved hurting someone else, but she would give no further details. We agreed to call the event the 'G-factor'. I spoke in general terms about tackling guilt and recommended a self-help book (Dryden 1994c), then we focused on problems she did want to reveal.

At a three-month follow-up appointment, she said that her guilt had much reduced – 'It's a great weight off my mind' – because she absorbed and acted on the information from myself and the self-help book, but she still would not reveal what the problem was and I did not press the point. The problem had been resolved to her satisfaction and relief, which was the key issue.

'yes, but . . .' thinking

This can be a particularly frustrating form of client response as it indicates the need for change, then negates it with the 'but'. Burns (1981) suggests using the 'BUT-REBUTTAL' method whereby each client 'but' (e.g. 'I do want to ask someone out, but I'm worried about being rejected') elicits a rebuttal from you (e.g. 'You might be rejected, but, on the other hand, you might get lucky'). The idea is to challenge each 'but' until the client runs out of them and makes a COMMITMENT to change. While this technique can be useful at times, it can also degenerate at other times into an unproductive 'battle of the buts'. Another method is to respond to the 'yes' and ignore the 'but':

Client: Yes, it does make sense to tell my partner that I think our sex life is a bit dull, but he might get upset and that will cause problems.

Therapist: So you ask your partner to spice up the sex and then what?

Client: Yes, that would be exciting if he could do that, but he might think he isn't satisfying me.

Therapist: What would that mean for the relationship if your sex life was more exciting?

Client: Well, a better time both in and out of bed. Put more fun into the relationship like it used to be and bring us closer together again, but, of course, it could backfire with him getting all moody and stand-offish and thinking I don't love him any more.

Therapist: So is improving the sex and the relationship worth striving for?

Client: Yes, definitely, but . . . have you been listening to me?

You can point out that you have been listening to the part of her that wants change in the relationship while she has been listening to the part of herself that worries about the consequences of 'speaking up' for her desires. 'Yes' seeks to change the status quo while 'but' maintains it.

'you haven't been there'

Some clients believe that if 'you haven't been there' (i.e. experienced similar problems to theirs) then you cannot understand what they have been through. Your empathy will be based on theory, not a shared experience of 'hitting rock bottom'. The 'you haven't been there' retort is particularly prevalent among substance abusers. Some of these clients may have been in therapy before with former addicts-turned-counsellors but this did not make much of an impact on them as they quickly relapsed. What, then, is the crucial importance of the therapist 'having been there' if it does not lead to constructive change in the client's life? While your knowledge of drink and drug abuse may come only from books and clients' accounts of their experiences, they can learn about the development and maintenance of their problems from the cognitive model of substance use (Liese and Franz 1996).

A variation on the 'you haven't been there' argument is that 'you would have been there' if you had the client's life or been in the situations he has. In other words, substance abuse would have been the inevitable outcome for you. You can observe, without being arrogant or patronizing, that it would not have been inevitable because there are other ways of seeing the same situation (which is what you want to teach clients in CBT):

- Considering the adverse consequences of substance abuse and therefore avoiding getting involved in it. Longer-term thinking prevailing over instant gratification.
- Resisting peer pressure and seeing nothing intrinsically desirable about getting 'wrecked'.
- Understanding that psychological problems are best addressed with a clear head and without creating additional problems in the process.

You might want to use SELF-DISCLOSURE to show clients that even in 'rock bottom' times in your life you did not resort to substance abuse (if this is true) because you wanted to get yourself off 'the bottom', not left on it, and looked for effective problem-solving methods. We think it creates a false empathy to try and communicate to the client 'there but for the grace of God go I. I suppose I was just lucky not to get into it' when substance abuse never had any appeal for you. The therapeutic relationship should be based on honesty, not ingratiation.

zigzag

When clients formulate their new adaptive beliefs, they will also mount attacks on these beliefs as their maladaptive beliefs are still powerfully held. These new beliefs are easily destabilized by these attacks as clients usually have, at this stage in the change process, only weak conviction in their new beliefs. Instead of your clients attempting to undermine these beliefs outside of the session or in 'secret', encourage them to use the sessions to both attack and defend these beliefs. The zigzag method of attack–response helps clients to improve their skills in self-debate – probably the most important factor in successful self-therapy. An example of the zigzag method is shown on the opposite page.

When your clients gain competence in using the zigzag method, encourage them to make their attacks and responses as vigorous as possible. The object of the exercise is for clients to strengthen their conviction in their adaptive beliefs and weaken their conviction in their maladaptive beliefs, not to have an altercation with themselves for the sake of it. Therefore, when the attacks peter out, clients should stop the exercise.

Adaptive belief
My boyfriend does not have to agree
with my opinions. We can agree to
disagree.

Attack
If he loved me, then he would
see things my way.

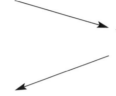

Response
I am joining together two separate
issues: our disagreements and
his love.

Attack
He could agree with me even if
he doesn't mean it.

Response
Then he would be patronizing me.
I don't want to be treated like a
frail flower. I want to know his real
views, not phoney ones.

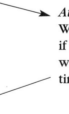

Attack
What's wrong with pretending
if it makes me happy? I don't
want damned honesty all the
time!

Response
I'm going to be firm about this: I want
our relationship to be based on
openness, honesty and mutual
respect. If I want to be treated like a
baby, then I'll get myself a pram and
a rattle!

References

Adler A (1964) Social Interest: A Challenge to Mankind. New York: Capricorn.

Alford BA, Beck AT (1997) The Integrative Power of Cognitive Therapy. New York: Guilford.

Antony MM, Swinson RP (1998) When Perfect Isn't Good Enough. Oakland, CA: New Harbinger Publications.

Appleyard B (2001) Barrymore's Diana syndrome. The Sunday Times (News Review), June 10.

Arnold J, Cooper CL, Robertson IT (1998) Work Psychology, 3rd edn. London: Pitman.

Bandura A (1977) Self-efficacy: Toward a unifying theory of behavioral change. Psychological Review 84: 191–215.

Baron J, Baron JH, Barber JP, Nolen-Hoekseman S (1990) Rational thinking as a goal of therapy. Journal of Cognitive Psychotherapy 4(3): 293–302.

Beck AT (1976) Cognitive Therapy and the Emotional Disorders. New York: International Universities Press.

Beck AT (1989) Love is Never Enough. New York: Penguin.

Beck AT, Rush AJ, Shaw BF, Emery G (1979) Cognitive Therapy of Depression. New York: Guilford.

Beck AT, Emery G, Greenberg RL (1985a) Anxiety Disorders and Phobias: A Cognitive Perspective. New York: Basic Books.

Beck AT, Steer RA, Kovacs M, Garrison B (1985b) Hopelessness and eventual suicide: a ten-year prospective study of patients hospitalized with suicidal ideation. American Journal of Psychiatry 142(5): 559–63.

Beck AT, Freeman A and Associates (1990) Cognitive Therapy of Personality Disorders. New York: Guilford.

Beck AT, Wright FD, Newman CF, Liese BS (1993) Cognitive Therapy of Substance Abuse. New York: Guilford.

Beck JS (1995) Cognitive Therapy: Basics and Beyond. New York: Guilford.

Berlin I (1998) From hope and fear set free. In Hardy H, Hausheer R (eds), The Proper Study of Mankind: An Anthology of Essays of Isaiah Berlin. London: Pimlico.

Bishay NR, Tarrier N, Dolan M, Beckett R, Harwood S (1996) Morbid jealousy: a cognitive outlook. Journal of Cognitive Psychotherapy 10(1): 9–22.

Blackburn IM, Davidson K (1995) Cognitive Therapy for Depression and Anxiety, amended. Oxford: Blackwell Scientific Publications.

Brammer L (1990) Teaching personal problem solving to adults. Journal of Cognitive Psychotherapy 4(3): 267–79.

Burns DD (1981) Feeling Good: The New Mood Therapy. New York: Signet.

Burns DD (1989) The Feeling Good Handbook. New York: William Morrow.

Butler G, Hope T (1996) Manage Your Mind. Oxford: Oxford University Press.

Butler G, McManus F (1998) Psychology: A Very Short Introduction. Oxford: Oxford University Press.

Clark DM (1989) Anxiety states. In Hawton K, Salkovskis PM, Kirk J, Clark DM (eds), Cognitive Behaviour Therapy for Psychiatric Problems. Oxford: Oxford University Press.

Cormier WH, Cormier LS (1985) Interviewing Strategies for Helpers. Monterey, CA: Brooks/Cole.

Davidson K (2000) Cognitive Therapy for Personality Disorders. London: Butterworth-Heinemann.

De Botton A. (2001) The Consolations of Philosophy. London: Penguin.

DiGiuseppe R (1991) Comprehensive cognitive disputing in RET. In Bernard ME (ed.), Using Rational-Emotive Therapy Effectively: A Practitioner's Guide. New York: Plenum.

Dowd ET (1996) Resistance and reactance in cognitive therapy. International Cognitive Therapy Newsletter 10(3): 3–5.

Dreikurs R (1968) Psychology in the Classroom, 2nd edn. New York: Harper and Row.

Dryden W (1985) Cognition without ignition. Contemporary Psychology 30(10): 788–89.

Dryden W (1994a) Progress in Rational Emotive Behaviour Therapy. London: Whurr.

Dryden W (1994b) 10 Steps to Positive Living. London: Sheldon Press.

Dryden W (1994c) Overcoming Guilt. London: Sheldon Press.

Dryden W (1995) Brief Rational Emotive Behaviour Therapy. Chichester: Wiley.

Dryden W (1997) Overcoming Shame. London: Sheldon Press.

Dryden W (1998) Developing Self-Acceptance. Chichester: Wiley.

Dryden W (2001) Reason to Change: A Rational Emotive Behaviour Therapy (REBT) Workbook. Hove, East Sussex: Brunner-Routledge.

Dryden W, Gordon J (1993a) Beating the Comfort Trap. London: Sheldon Press.

Dryden W, Gordon J (1993b) Peak Performance: Become More Effective at Work. Didcot, Oxfordshire: Mercury Business Books.

Dryden W, Gordon J (1994) How to Cope When the Going Gets Tough. London: Sheldon Press.

Dryden W, Neenan M (1995) Dictionary of Rational Emotive Behaviour Therapy. London: Whurr.

Dryden W, Yankura J (1995) Developing Rational Emotive Behavioural Counselling. London: Sage.

D'Zurilla TJ (1990) Problem-solving training for effective stress management and prevention. Journal of Cognitive Psychotherapy 4(4): 327–54.

Elliott KJ (1995) The WILFY method: unlearning lessons from the past. Journal of Cognitive Psychotherapy 9(4): 259–66.

Ellis A (1972) Helping people to get better rather than merely feel better. Rational Living 7(2): 2–9.

Ellis A (1979) The issue of force and energy in behavioral change. Journal of Contemporary Psychotherapy 10(2): 83–97.

Ellis A (1980) An overview of the clinical theory of rational-emotive therapy. In Grieger R, Boyd J (eds), Rational-Emotive Therapy: A Skills-Based Approach. New York: Van Nostrand Reinhold.

Ellis A (1983) The Case against Religiosity. New York: Albert Ellis Institute for Rational Emotive Behavior Therapy.

Ellis A (1984) How to Maintain and Enhance your Rational-Emotive Therapy Gains. New York: Albert Ellis Institute for Rational Emotive Behavior Therapy.

Ellis A (1985) Overcoming Resistance. New York: Springer.

Ellis A (2001) Feeling Better, Getting Better, Staying Better. Atascadero, CA: Impact Publishers.

Ellis A, McInerney JF, DiGiuseppe R, Yeager RJ (1988) Rational-Emotive Therapy with Alcoholics and Substance Abusers. New York: Pergamon.

Emery G (2000) Overcoming Depression. Oakland, CA: New Harbinger Publications.

Feltham C, Dryden W (1993) Dictionary of Counselling. London: Whurr.

Fennell MJV (1989) Depression. In Hawton K, Salkovskis PM, Kirk J, Clark DM (eds), Cognitive Behaviour Therapy for Psychiatric Problems. Oxford: Oxford University Press.

Fennell M (1999) Overcoming Low Self-Esteem. London: Robinson.

Fleming S, Robinson PJ (1991) The application of cognitive therapy to the bereaved. In Vallis TM, Howes JL, Miller PC (eds), The Challenge of Cognitive Therapy. New York: Plenum.

Flew A (1975) Thinking about Thinking. London: Fontana.

Forward S. (1997) Emotional Blackmail. London: Bantam Books.

Frank JD, Frank JB (1991) Persuasion and Healing, 3rd edn. Baltimore, MD: Johns Hopkins University Press.

Frankl VE (1985) Man's Search for Meaning. New York: Washington Square Press.

Free ML (1999) Cognitive Therapy in Groups. Chichester: Wiley.

Freeman A, Fusco G (2000) Treating high arousal patients: differentiating between patients in crisis and crisis-prone patients. In Dattilio FM, Freeman A (eds), Cognitive-Behavioural Strategies in Crisis Intervention, 2nd edn. New York: Guilford.

Frisch MB (1992) Use of the quality of life inventory in problem assessment and treatment planning for cognitive therapy of depression. In Freeman A, Dattilio FM (eds), Comprehensive Casebook of Cognitive Therapy. New York: Plenum.

Gantz FE, Gallagher-Thompson D, Rodman JL (1992) Inhibited grief. In Freeman A, Dattilio FM (eds), Comprehensive Casebook of Cognitive Therapy. New York: Plenum.

Gilbert P (1992) Depression: The Evolution of Powerlessness. New York: Guilford.

Gilbert P (1997) Overcoming Depression. London: Robinson.

Gilbert P (2000) Counselling for Depression, 2nd edn. London: Sage.

Glover M (1988) Responsibility and therapy. In Dryden W, Trower P (eds), Developments in Cognitive Psychotherapy. London: Sage.

Greenberger D (1992) The suicidal patient. In Freeman A, Dattilio FM (eds), Comprehensive Casebook of Cognitive Therapy. New York: Plenum.

Greenberger D, Padesky CA (1995) Mind over Mood. New York: Guilford.

Grieger RM (1991) Keys to effective RET. In Bernard ME (ed.), Using Rational-Emotive Therapy Effectively: A Practitioner's Guide. New York: Plenum.

Grieger RM, Boyd J (1980) Rational-Emotive Therapy: A Skills-Based Approach. New York: Van Nostrand Reinhold.

Hauck P (1966) The neurotic agreement in psychotherapy. Rational Living 1(1): 32–35.

Hauck P (1974) Depression. London: Sheldon Press.

Hauck P (1980a) Brief Counseling with RET. Philadelphia, PA: Westminster Press.

Hauck P (1980b) Calm Down. London: Sheldon Press.

Hauck P (1981) Why Be Afraid? London: Sheldon Press.

Hauck P (1982a) Jealousy. London: Sheldon Press.

Hauck P (1982b) How To Do Want You Want To Do. London: Sheldon Press.

Hauck P (1983) How To Love and Be Loved. London: Sheldon Press.

Hauck P (1988) How To Be Your Own Best Friend. London: Sheldon Press.

Hauck P (1991a) RET and the assertive process. In Bernard ME (ed.), Using Rational-Emotive Therapy Effectively: A Practitioner's Guide. New York: Plenum.

Hauck P (1991b) Hold Your Head Up High. London: Sheldon Press.

Heppner PP (1990) Future directions of problem-solving training for adults. Journal of Cognitive Psychotherapy 4(4): 243–46.

Honey P, Mumford A (1992) The Manual of Learning Styles, 3rd edn. Maidenhead, Berkshire: Honey Publications.

Janoff-Bulman R (1992) Shattered Assumptions: Towards a New Psychology of Trauma. New York: Free Press.

Jones K (1998) Time Management. London: Marshall Publishing.

Kennerley H (2000) Overcoming Childhood Trauma. London: Robinson.

Kimmel J (1976) The rational barb in the treatment of social rejection. Rational Living 11: 23–25.

Kleinke CL (1991) Coping with Life Challenges. Pacific Grove, CA: Brooks/Cole.

Knaus WJ (1993) Overcoming procrastination. In Bernard ME, Wolfe JL (eds), The RET Resource Book for Practitioners. New York: Albert Ellis Institute for Rational Emotive Behavior Therapy.

Knaus WJ (1998) Do It Now! 2nd edn. New York: Wiley.

Kolb DA (1984) Experiential Learning. Englewood Cliffs, NJ: Prentice-Hall.

Kubany ES (1998) Cognitive therapy for trauma-related guilt. In Follette VM, Ruzek JI, Abueg FR (eds,) Cognitive-Behavioural Therapies for Trauma. New York: Guilford.

Lazarus AA, Lazarus C, Fay A (1993) Don't Believe It For a Minute: Forty Toxic Ideas That Are Driving You Crazy. Atascadero, CA: Impact Publishers.

Lazarus RS (1999) Stress and Emotion. London: Free Association Books.

Leahy RL (1996) Cognitive Therapy: Basic Principles and Applications. Northvale, NJ: Jason Aronson Inc.

Leahy RL (2001) Overcoming Resistance in Cognitive Therapy. New York: Guilford.

Leahy RL, Holland SJ (2000) Treatment Plans and Interventions for Depression and Anxiety Disorders. New York: Guilford.

Lerner MJ (1980) The Belief in a Just World: A Fundamental Delusion. New York: Plenum.

Liese BS, Franz RA (1996) Treating substance use disorders with cognitive therapy: lessons learned and implications for the future. In Salkovskis PM (ed.), Frontiers of Cognitive Therapy. New York: Guilford.

Magee B (1982) Men of Ideas. Oxford: Oxford University Press.

Mann S (1999) Hiding What We Feel, Faking What We Don't. Shaftesbury, Dorset: Element Books.

Mathews TJ (2000) The cross and the Christian client. The Rational Emotive Behaviour Therapist 8(1): 10–14.

Maultsby MC (1975) Help Yourself to Happiness. New York: Albert Ellis Institute for Rational Emotive Behavior Therapy.

McKay M, Davis M, Fanning P (1997) Thoughts and Feelings, 2nd edn. Oakland, CA: New Harbinger Publications.

McMullin RE (1986) Handbook of Cognitive Therapy Techniques. New York: Norton.

Naugle AE, Follette WC (1998) A functional analysis of trauma symptoms. In Follette VM, Ruzek JI, Abueg FR (eds), Cognitive-Behavioral Therapies for Trauma. New York: Guilford.

Neenan M, Dryden W (1996) Dealing with Difficulties in Rational Emotive Behaviour Therapy. London: Whurr.

Neenan M, Dryden W (1999) Rational Emotive Behaviour Therapy: Advances in Theory and Practice. London: Whurr.

Neenan M, Dryden W (2000a) Essential Cognitive Therapy. London: Whurr.

Neenan M, Dryden W (2000b) Essential Rational Emotive Behaviour Therapy. London: Whurr.

Neenan M, Dryden W (2001) Learning from Errors in Rational Emotive Behaviour Therapy. London: Whurr.

Neenan M, Dryden W (2002) Life Coaching: A Cognitive Behavioural Approach. London: Brunner-Routledge.

Newman CF (2000) Hypotheticals in cognitive psychotherapy: creative questions, novel answers, and therapeutic change. Journal of Cognitive Psychotherapy 14(2): 135-47.

Nezu AM, Nezu CM, Lombardo ER (2001) Managing stress through problem solving. Stress News, Journal of the International Stress Management Association (UK) 13(3): 11-14.

Padesky CA (1993a) Schema as self-prejudice. International Cognitive Therapy Newsletter 5/6: 16-17.

Padesky CA (1993b) Staff and patient education. In Wright JH, Thase ME, Beck AT, Ludgate JW (eds), Cognitive Therapy with Inpatients. New York: Guilford.

Padesky CA (1994) Schema change processes in cognitive therapy. Clinical Psychology and Psychotherapy 1(5): 267-78.

Padesky CA, Greenberger D (1995) Clinician's Guide to Mind over Mood. New York: Guilford.

Persons JB (1989) Cognitive Therapy in Practice: A Case Formulation Approach. New York: Norton.

Platt JJ, Prout MF, Metzger DS (1986) Interpersonal cognitive problem-solving therapy. In Dryden W, Golden W (eds), Cognitive-Behavioural Approaches to Psychotherapy. London: Harper and Row.

Priest G (2000) Logic: A Very Short Introduction. Oxford: Oxford University Press.

Quick JC, Quick JD, Nelson DL, Hurrell Jr JJ (eds) (1997) Preventive Stress Management in Organizations, 2nd edn. Washington, DC: American Psychological Association.

Robb HB (1992) Why you don't have a 'perfect right' to anything. Journal of Rational-Emotive and Cognitive-Behavior Therapy 10(4): 259-70.

Rorer LG (1999) Dealing with the intellectual-insight problem in cognitive and rational emotive behavior therapy. Journal of Rational-Emotive and Cognitive-Behavior Therapy 17(4): 217-36.

Rudd MD, Joiner T, Rajab MH (2001) Treating Suicidal Behavior. New York: Guilford.

Salkovskis PM (1996) The cognitive approach to anxiety: threat beliefs, safety-seeking behavior, and the special case of health anxiety and obsessions. In Salkovskis PM (ed.), Frontiers of Cognitive Therapy. New York: Guilford.

Salkovskis PM, Bass C (1997) Hypochondriasis. In Clark DM, Fairburn CG (eds), Science and Practice of Cognitive Behaviour Therapy. Oxford: Oxford University Press.

Schuyler D (1991) A Practical Guide to Cognitive Therapy. New York: Norton.

Sheldon B (1995) Cognitive-Behavioural Therapy. London: Routledge.

Shneidman E (1985) Definition of Suicide. New York: Wiley.

Storr A (1997) Feet of Clay: A Study of Gurus. London: HarperCollins.

Strohmer DC, Blustein DL (1990) The adult problem solver as person scientist. Journal of Cognitive Psychotherapy 4(3): 281–92.

Walen SR, DiGiuseppe R, Dryden W (1992) A Practitioner's Guide to Rational-Emotive Therapy, 2nd edn. New York: Oxford University Press.

Warburton N (2000) Thinking from A to Z, 2nd edn. London: Routledge.

Warren R, Zgourides GD (1991) Anxiety Disorders: A Rational-Emotive Perspective. New York: Pergamon.

Wasik B (1984) Teaching Parents Effective Problem-Solving: A Handbook for Professionals. Unpublished manuscript. Chapel Hill: University of North Carolina.

Weishaar ME (1993) Aaron T. Beck. London: Sage.

Wells A (1997) Cognitive Therapy of Anxiety Disorders. Chichester: Wiley.

Wessler RL (1986) Conceptualizing cognitions in the cognitive-behavioural therapies. In Dryden W, Golden WL (eds), Cognitive-Behavioural Approaches to Psychotherapy. London: Harper and Row.

Wessler RA, Wessler RL (1980) The Principles and Practice of Rational-Emotive Therapy. San Francisco, CA: Jossey-Bass.

White CA (2001) Cognitive Behaviour Therapy for Chronic Medical Problems. Chichester: Wiley.

Wills F, Sanders D (1997) Cognitive Therapy: Transforming the Image. London: Sage.

Worden JW (1982) Grief Counseling and Grief Therapy. New York: Springer.

Young HS (1988) Teaching rational self-value concepts to tough customers. In Dryden W, Trower P (eds), Developments in Rational-Emotive Therapy. Open University Press: Milton Keynes.

Zuercher-White E (1999) Overcoming Panic Disorder and Agoraphobia. Oakland, CA: New Harbinger.